By the same author
MODERN UPHOLSTERY

The
Modern Lampshade Book

DOROTHY COX

Illustrated by Denise Cox

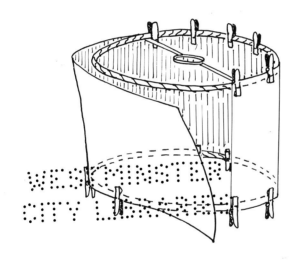

LONDON   G. BELL & SONS, LTD

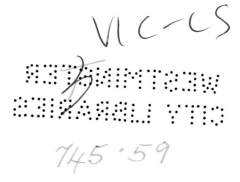

VIC-CS

745·59

ISBN 0 7135 1763 8 /7801

Contents

Photographs

Introduction

Lampshade making is one of the most popular crafts, and a little reflection reveals several reasons for this popularity.

It is a craft which allows a novice, who is prepared to give a little time and care to his or her work, to produce an article which reaches a very high standard of finish—an article which has no suggestion of looking 'homemade'.

It is a craft which allows a devotee to experiment and become an expert who can produce work which is quite original and of a high degree of excellence.

This craft is only a section of the much wider craft of Soft Furnishing and an essential part of the art of interior decoration. These arts have never aroused more interest in every type of home than they do today. Practically every housewife and very many men take a great interest in making their homes attractive and comfortable places in which to live.

The ability to make lampshades enables one to be sure that the shades tie up with the décor in any particular room. They should not be things apart, but an integral part of the whole scheme. They can complement the colour scheme in a room, they can bring a fabric to different parts of a room. An example, Plate 25, shows shades using the material of the curtains and dressing table drapes. Plate 24 shows a shade using the same material as that used for a waste-paper bin, a tissue holder and cushion, and so linking up a number of small articles.

Attractive commercial lampshades are expensive to buy, whereas a homemade lampshade is very economical to make. Browsing round the lampshade department of large stores or visiting specialist shops will confirm the truth of this statement and at the same time enable one to keep abreast with modern styles and fashion trends in this craft. The high cost of the commercial shades can be readily understood when it is realised that the shades are almost completely handmade. As with all crafts it is the labour which makes the finished article expensive, but with homemade articles we do not consider the time which has been expended. The quantities of fabric used in many lampshades are very small and do not involve great expense.

Complete originality in one's home is the reward of the craftworker. By varying the materials used and the combination or treatment of these materials or by introducing a second craft (Chapter 28), shades are achieved, the like of which cannot be seen in any other home.

In these days of shortage of time—in spite of extra leisure—it is heartening to find a craft in which a completed article is achieved in a comparatively short space of time. This factor, together with the small outlay of money, enables anyone, by making one or more new lamp-

viii

shades, to give a facelift and new lease of life to a room which is losing its freshness and failing to make an impact on its users.

Lampshade making is one of our newer crafts, and so there are no traditional techniques which must be observed. Thus the worker is completely free to experiment, both with materials and methods, choosing those which give the most attractive and easily achieved result. Even though this is a comparatively young craft, already rethinking has occurred about some of the techniques and materials used (pages 8, 16 and 17).

No other branch of soft furnishing is more sensitive to fashion changes and practically each year brings fresh designs in frames. This is an ideal situation as fresh challenges are being presented to the worker which prevent the craft becoming merely one of repetition.

Acknowledgements

The writing of this book has only been made possible by the generous co-operation of many people. They have given unstintingly of their time and advice and I would like to express my sincere thanks to:

Mrs. Denise Cox for her help and patience with the illustrations, also to Mr. Gill and Mr. Barke for their assistance in this field.

George Wostenholm & Co. of Sheffield, who provided the original sketches of the various types of scissors.

Mr. & Mrs. A. H. Parfitt for their interest and patience when taking the photographs.

My students who loaned their lampshades for photographs and who were so willing to experiment with new ideas. In particular I would like to thank all those who worked with me to provide the examples for the chapter 'Try a New Craft'.

Finally my family and colleagues for their practical help in checking the scripts and for their encouragement with the whole project. In particular Mrs. Olive Cox for the considerable time she has spent helping me to make up the shades.

January, 1973   U.D.C.

I

Buying the Frame and Equipment

WHEN deciding to make a lampshade there are many factors to be considered:

(a) The purpose of the shade. Is it to be strictly functional, to transmit the maximum amount of light?—or is it to be mainly decortive?—or possibly combine these roles? Both the size and the shape of the frame are factors which influence the amount of light thrown into the room (Figures 1a and b, 2a and b).

(b) The room in which it is to be sited. The size and the height of the room must be considered. Small pendant shades appear out of proportion in large rooms. Coolie shades are very useful when ceiling lights are required for low rooms or possibly on beams (Plate 5), oval shades are ideal for reading lamps standing on shelves.

(c) The type of material to be used for the cover. Firm materials usually only require two rings; one with a fitting (see page 3) and one plain ring. Frames to be covered by soft materials must have two rings at least separated by struts which prevent the shade from collapsing like a concertina.

(d) When using soft fabrics or introducing a second craft (Chapter 28) the nature, texture, amount of give and the design of the material will each have an influence on the style and the shape of frame chosen; for example, a bowed drum must be covered with material which can be used on the cross, (Plates 2Aa and c). Striped material and most embroidery must be fitted on the straight. (Plates 17, 19 and 23).

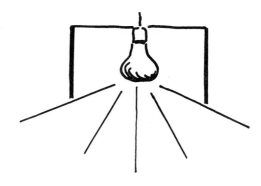

Fig. 1a Shallow drum allows the light to spread

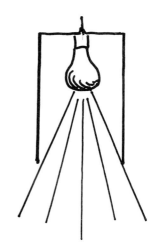

Fig. 1b Tall, narrow drum restricts the area lit

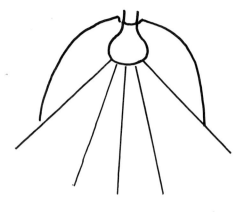

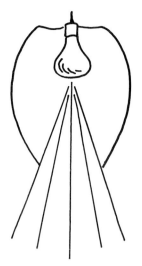

Fig. 2a Open Tiffany illuminates wide area

Fig. 2b Tulip Tiffany illuminates restricted area

(e) The other furnishings in the room. Are they modern or traditional? Drums, round or oval, bowed or straight-sided, fit well into modern schemes, whereas the more traditional schemes are suitable backgrounds for empire shades. These are only general guides, as other factors such as the type of material used for the cover will modify this factor.

(f) The way in which the covering fabric is to be used, e.g. when pleating. If the pleats are to be swathed a bowed frame should be used; if the struts are straight an angular broken effect is obtained. On the other hand if straight pleats are to be made then the frame should have straight struts.

(g) The base on which the shade is to fit. Before any work is begun on the frame, it should be tested on the base to ensure that a balanced effect is obtained. It is not always possible to take the base to the shop when buying the frame, but most shops are willing to exchange undamaged frames. It is not easy to give a general rule regarding the relationship between the size of the frame and that of the base as the style of the frame —see also Fig. 3—can give an optical illu-

sion, e.g. an 8″ drum appears quite a lot larger than an 8″ bowed empire and so could be used on a larger base (Figure 3).

(h) The size of the bulb to be used under the shade. With all types of material air must be able to circulate freely around the bulb to prevent scorching. The shades in Plate 5 have been in use for six years and show no signs of discolouration by the heat transmitted by the bulb.

(i) The time that the worker has available to devote to the making of the shade. Obviously the firm shades are generally more quickly made than the soft-fabric ones, and the pleated covers take longer than the tailored styles, although they are not necessarily more difficult.

From the above factors it will readily be appreciated that frames can be divided into 'types', i.e. according to the type of fitting they have, and by 'style', i.e. their shape, the latter being affected by current fashion. Usually each style can be obtained with any of the different fittings (see page 3).

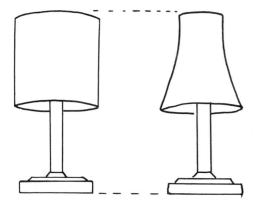

Fig. 3 Showing the different effect of using two styles of frame which are the 'same size'—the lower rings having the same diameter

TYPES OF FITTING

(1) *Pendant Fitting.* (Figure 4a) This type is used for hanging shades. In the centre of the top ring is a small ring which fits onto the adapter and this small ring is joined by two shoulders to the top ring.

(2) *Dropped Pendant.* (Figure 4b) This type is often found on true drums or rings to be used with firm materials. It can be used for hanging shades or for reading lamps. In the latter case the frame is simply inverted and the fact that the fitting is raised ensures that the bulb holder is hidden, always an important consideration.

(3) *Gimbal Fitting.* (Figure 4c) This type of fitting is designed for use on a table lamp. The hinged gimbal allows the shade to be tilted to direct the light in any specific direction. Care must be taken when tilting the shade to see that the cover does not touch the lamp bulb or scorching will occur. The fact that the gimbal is hinged should not be used to convert the shade into a pendant type as is sometimes suggested. The hinge appears very ugly when viewed from below;

also a gimbal frame is more expensive than its pendant counterpart.

(4) *Duplex Fitting.* (Figure 4d) This fitting is on frames or rings designed to be used on standard lamps or very large table lamps. There is a smaller inner ring attached to the top ring by three or four shoulders, and this smaller ring is several inches below the top ring and it sits on a shade carrier. This construction means that the bulb will be in the middle of the shade so that the maximum amount of light will be reflected and a well balanced shade obtained.

(5) *Butterfly Clip.* (Figure 4e) These are found on small shades to be used on wall fittings or multiple ceiling fittings, when the bulb faces upwards.

Rings or frames with struts can be found in all the above fittings.

(6) *Bedhead Fitting.* (Figure 4f) This is designed to hook onto a bedhead and so the light is reflected downwards to facilitate reading in bed.

3

Fig. 4a. Pendant fitting
for hanging shades.

Fig. 4b. Dropped, or recessed, pendant
for hanging or reading lights.

Fig. 4c. Gimbal fitting
for reading lamps.

Fig. 4d. Duplex fitting and shade carrier for standard lamps.

Fig. 4e. Butterfly clip
for small shades.

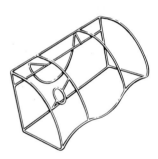

Fig. 4f. Bedhead fitting.

STYLES OF SHADES

It is in the style of a frame that the effect of fashion is seen. It dictates the frames which are to be found in the shops at any particular time. Some styles remain constantly popular and are always available, as is the case with the bowed empire (Figure 4c). A few years ago drum shades (Figure 5a), both round and oval, became very much used (and very soon variations of the style appeared, e.g. the bowed drum and the angular drum (Figure 5b). (Plates 2Aa and c, and 2Bb). Coolie shades had a period of popularity and then became less common although they still have a very definite value (see page 1). The Tiffany frame is a current favourite and already its variations are on the market (Plates 12a and 12b and Figure 5d). Other styles, such as rectangular frames with cutaway or indented corners, offer variety and a challenge to the worker (Plate 11).

It is often frustrating that exciting and unusual frames which are seen made up in the high class shops are never available to the home worker. There are some specialist shops to be found and a visit to these will be very rewarding. Frames, because of their fragile nature, are difficult to pack and so a personal visit is usually necessary. Alternatively, it is occasionally possible to find a craftsman who is willing to make frames from sketches. These are obviously more expensive, but for the ambitious and adventurous they are well worth the extra cost.

Frames are made from copper or steel wire and the gauge or thickness of the wire used varies according to the size of the frame. It is important that the wire should be sufficiently thick to give the frame stability and to withstand the considerable strain exerted on it during the fitting of the cover and lining. Other points to check are the security of the welding where the struts join the rings and the sharpness of the ends of the struts. (See preparation of frame, page 8). Always stand the frame on a flat surface and test it for rocking and view it for symmetry.

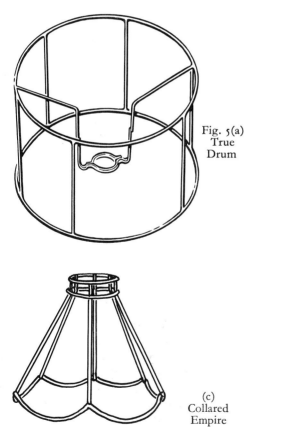

Fig. 5(a)
True
Drum

(c)
Collared
Empire

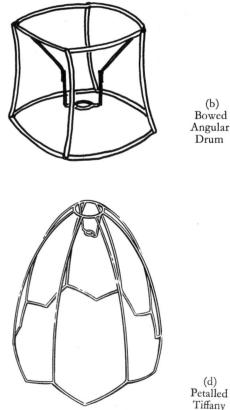

(b)
Bowed
Angular
Drum

(d)
Petalled
Tiffany

5

Pins. Small, fine pins should be used as they are less likely to leave pin-marks in the fabric after fitting has been completed. Long pins are much more likely to scratch the worker and draw blood, so marking the fabrics. Large numbers of pins are frequently in use at the same time (as in a pleated shade) and the smaller they are the better especially when the cover is being stitched into position. Occasionally with very fine fabrics brass lace-pins can be used. A few glass-headed pins are useful as marker pins (Figure 35). The small pins are usually sold under the name of 'Lillikins' or 'Lills'.

Needles. For the majority of stitching short, stiff needles known as 'betweens' are ideal—No. 5 and 6 thicknesses, as they are less likely to bend or break when they strike the frame. A packet of mixed sizes and a small curved needle will also be useful for various specialist tasks. Once a needle has been used for lampshade making it should NOT be used for any other needlework as it will be blunted by striking the frame. The working needle should be changed when it has lost its point otherwise it will pull the threads.

Scissors. As with all crafts using soft fabrics, sharp scissors are essential. Two pairs are necessary; a large pair of dressmaking scissors (Figure 6a) for cutting the fabric and a fine pair for trimming away surplus material. Vine or surgical scissors (Figures 6c and 6e) are ideal for this trimming but embroidery scissors (Figure 6b) can be used successfully. A special pair of scissors should be used for cutting firm materials as these will blunt dressmaking scissors; some kitchen scissors are ideal for this task (Figure 6d).

Thimble. This is a 'must'. Even if one has never used a thimble in one's life, anybody

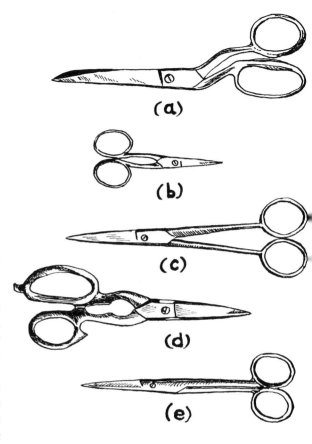

Fig. 6a. Dressmaker's scissors for cutting out.
Fig. 6b. Embroidery scissors.
Fig. 6c. Grape scissors.
Fig. 6d. Kitchen scissors for firm fabrics.
Fig. 6e. Surgical scissors for neat trimming.

who starts to make a lampshade will soon be converted to its usefulness. If the frame has been well bound it is, or should be, quite difficult to push pins and needles through the binding and a painful hole will soon

6

appear in the end of the finger if a thimble is not worn.

Threads. These should match the materials being used, both in colour and texture. The transparent nylon thread which is available is very useful for attaching open trimmings such as metallic lace.

Other sewing aids such as tailor's chalk, tape measure, hem-guides, etc., which are found in most sewing boxes, will be used from time to time.

Tracing Wheel. This can be useful when reproducing panels for the lining (Chapter 8 and Figure 56).

Clothes pegs with a spring clip design are used instead of pins when fitting firm materials to rings (Figure 114b). They control this stiff type of material more firmly than pins which tend to tear such fabrics.

A metal file is used in the preparation of the frame when the sharp edges of the struts or rough joints have to be smoothed.

Light Diffusers have recently appeared on the market. They can be fitted to the lower ring of a shade so that the light from the bulb is diffused. They are particularly useful in very wide shades and when inserted they are level with the bottom of the shade.

Instant Tailor Tack Marker. This is a very useful small gadget which can be used for tailor tacking. It is obtained from haberdashery departments of most large stores. The pieces of material to be marked are placed over a thick blanket or piece of polyether foam rubber and the needle is pushed through the material into the padding and a line of tacking is produced. Thread and a spare needle are provided with each marker.

2

Preparation of the Frame

AS WITH so many crafts, it is the initial preparation which lays the foundation of success or paves the way to disappointment and frustration. With most frames it usually involves three processes:

 (a) smoothing any sharp edges or joints,
 (b) painting,
 (c) binding.

It is regarding the preparation of the frame that some rethinking has taken place during recent years. In the early days of the craft it was usual to bind the rings and all the struts. Present trends are to bind the struts only when it is necessary for one of the following reasons:

(a) For the construction of the shade—as when the cover is attached in sections or panels and therefore has to be stitched to the struts (Plates 7, 11, 13a and 15c).

(b) To improve the appearance of the finished shade—as with unlined shades, especially hanging shades and those with wide bases such as the Tiffany shades (Plate 12a and b). It is not always possible to find a paint which is a perfect match to the underside of the cover material and the struts may be less conspicuous in these circumstances if they are bound with a matching material (see page 10).

In addition the exposed paintwork may become chipped during use and rusting will then occur.

(c) When using a very sheer fabric for the cover as with some forms of pleating, the struts are less obvious if bound with strips of the chiffon, etc.

The reasons for this change of thought are twofold:

(i) elimination of unnecessary work.

(ii) binding the struts can produce ridged lines under a tailored cover. These can both collect dirt and spoil the smooth line of the cover. If it is necessary to bind the struts of an unlined shade referred to above then the binding must be very smooth (see binding—pages 10 and 11).

Both methods are correct and acceptable if well done: it is the finished appearance which is important.

SMOOTHING THE FRAME

Even if the frame has been carefully examined before purchase it will probably have some sharp ends to the struts or rough joins, which if left in this condition will cut through the cover or lining materials and prevent a really smooth line being achieved round the edge of the shade. They must be filed down very carefully. If a strut comes loose it is impossible for an amateur to refix it. The smoothing can easily be done with a bastard file and strong but careful strokes made bringing the file up and away from the frame (Figure 7).

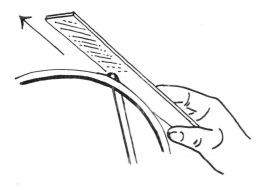

Fig. 7.

PAINTING

This is necessary to prevent the frame from rusting, either after washing or when used in a damp atmosphere. If this rusting occurs it will mark the covering fabric, spoiling its appearance and eventually causing it to rot.

A fast-drying cellulose paint or enamel are the most successful materials to use for this purpose. If the struts are to be visible, as in a shade without an internal lining, the paint should match the underside of the covering fabric or the external lining if one is used. The paint should be smoothly and evenly applied. Sufficient coats should be used to give the required depth of colour. A higher standard of finish is achieved if the whole frame, including the fitting, is painted. The fitting may appear bright initially, but many a shade has been spoiled by early discolouration of the fitting. Because of the very considerable friction of the fingers and the binding on the paintwork normal drying times do not always apply. The painting should be done at least two or three days before the frame is to be used.

COMMERCIALLY PREPARED FRAMES

It is possible to buy from some suppliers frames which are prepared ready for use. They have either been stove-enamelled or covered by a thin layer of plastic. The latter method does produce a rather bulky frame. Both types of frame are obviously more expensive than an unprepared frame. However for the worker who dislikes the messy preparation or has only a limited amount of time to devote to the craft the stove-enamelled frame is a real boon.

BINDING

For all soft-fabric-covered shades, here lies the secret of success. Any soft cover, other than one with an overskirt attached only to the top ring, should be drum-tight. This will only be achieved if the binding is so tight that it cannot twist or slip the merest fraction of an inch. If there is any doubt about the perfection of the binding it must be redone.

Various materials can be used for binding the rings and the struts. The one best suited to the particular shade being made should be chosen from tape, ribbon, Paris binding, strips of self-material, or bias-binding.

(a) *Tape.* This is almost always the most satisfactory to use when the binding will not be visible on the completed shade—as when an internal lining is inserted (see Chapter 6) or when the ring is completely covered by the trimming. Soft, household tape is the most useful; linen tape being too stiff to be moulded to the frame. $\frac{1}{4}''$ tape can be used where edge to edge binding is required (e.g. when struts have to be bound: Figure 9). $\frac{3}{8}''$ tape is ideal for binding the rings; this will overlap slightly (Figure 15), but for rings to which materials are to be sewn this is an advantage as it

9

gives a little more binding into which the needle can be inserted. Some handicraft shops sell a special soft lampshade tape, both in white and pastel colours. It is also possible to dye tape to match covering material if this is necessary.

(b) *Ribbon.* This is used exactly as tape. It is not quite as pliable as tape and hence requires a little more care, but it is available in a much wider range of colours. It is used when the binding will be visible on the finished shade.

(c) *Paris Binding.* Much the same as ribbon but with a more restricted range of widths.

(d) *Strips of material*, matching the lining or cover. This is highly successful when the binding is to be visible on the completed shade. It is, however, only practical with thin materials such as Jap silk or chiffon when a perfect match and a smooth surface can be achieved at the same time. Thick materials would give a binding which would be much too bulky. Selvedges are ideal for this type of binding if torn off $\frac{1}{2}''$ wide. When this is exhausted, strips $\frac{5}{8}''$ wide torn or cut on the straight of the fabric can be used and ONE edge ironed in for $\frac{1}{8}''$. The binding is then overlapped; the folded edge covering the raw edge (Figure 10).

(e) *Tape overbound* with sheer fabric, e.g. chiffon. This gives a very firm binding to which the cover may be stitched and yet it will match the cover. Obviously this is only necessary when the bound rings are to be visible (page 47), when an external lining only is used.

(f) *Bias-binding.* This is not an ideal material for binding, especially for soft-fabric shades, and should only be used if no other matching material is available and even then be restricted to struts. As it is cut on the cross it tends to stretch longer and longer and at the same time become narrower—it

may even break under the strain. It can be used with less risk for binding the rings used for firm shades. Here the binding does not affect the tautness of the cover. When bias-binding is used one edge must be ironed out and it is used as the strips in (d) above.

METHOD OF BINDING

When the struts are to be bound permanently, these are done first and then the rings are bound.

If it is desirable that the struts should not be bound permanently, the rings are bound first and then any strut to which the fabric is to be fitted (see Covers and Linings for Tailored Shades, Chapter 6). This binding on the struts may be removed after fitting is completed.

To Bind the Struts

Allow twice the length of a strut when using $\frac{1}{4}''$ tape or ribbon.

Allow one and a half times the length of a strut with any other binding material.

(1) Taper the end of the binding (Figures 8a and b)—this avoids bulk at the top of the strut. Place the end of the tape under the ring at the top of the strut.

(2) Bring the pointed end of the tape over the junction of the strut and the ring and bind in the pointed end (Figures 8a, b, and 9).

(3) Keeping the tape at a VERY ACUTE ANGLE to the strut, continue binding towards the lower ring. When using $\frac{1}{4}''$ tape or ribbon the binding will be edge to edge (Figure 9), with other types of binding it will slightly overlap (Figure 10).

(4) When the bottom ring is reached loop the binding round the ring at its junction with the strut (Figure 11). Leave any surplus binding untrimmed at this stage.

10

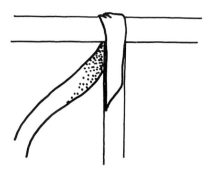

Fig. 8a To begin binding using tape, ribbon, Paris binding or selvedge

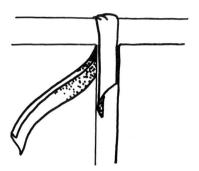

Fig. 8b To commence binding using strips of self-fabric

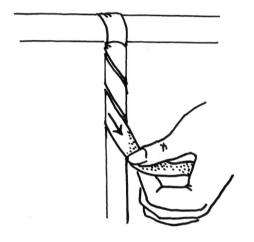

Figure 9.

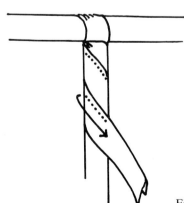

Figure 10.

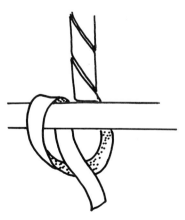

Figure 11.

11

To Bind the Rings

Allow twice the circumference of the ring.
Top Ring: (1) Taper the end of the binding.
Place the pointed end under the ring at the
top of the strut (Figure 12).

(2) Bring the tape over the junction of the
ring and the strut and bind in the pointed
end. Keeping the binding at an ACUTE
ANGLE, and allowing it to overlap slightly,
continue to the top of the next strut (Figures
13, 14).

(3) At the top of each strut bind right up
to the junction of the ring and the strut and
put in one extra wrap (Figures 15–17) and
carry on to the next strut (Figure 17). The
extra wrap ensures that the top of the strut is
completely covered and at the same time
allows the binding to continue at a very
acute angle to the frame. It is also very much
less bulky than the result of making a figure
of '8'. This last method—the figure of '8'—
(Figures 18a, b, c, d,) is very occasionally
the more successful; this is usually where
there is a sharp point (Figure 5d—the petal
Tiffany). Experience and experimenting will
reveal the best method in any difficult cir-
cumstance.

(4) When the binding is complete, stitch
the END of the binding to the BEGINNING
(Figure 19). This is most important to prevent the binding slipping back round the
ring. Pin the join before stitching and test
the tightness of the binding (see page 9). If
there is the slightest suggestion of the
binding moving it must be redone or it will
be impossible to get a really tight cover.
Stitch on the outside of the ring with small
stitches (Figure 19). If the stitches are on
the outside of the ring they will always be
covered by the cover, even though there is
no lining. Trim off any surplus binding.

Note: The raw edge is NOT turned in.

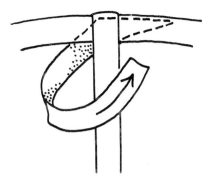

Fig. 12

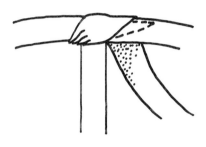

Fig. 13

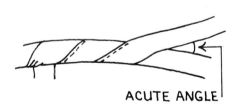

ACUTE ANGLE

Fig. 14

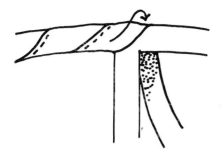

Fig. 15

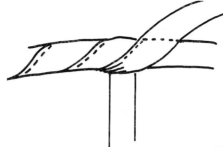

Fig. 16

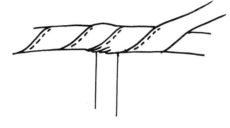

Fig. 17

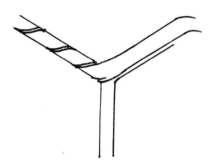

Fig. 18a

Fig. 18b

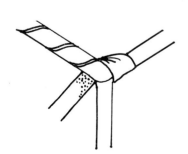

Fig. 18c

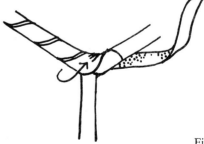

Fig. 18d

13

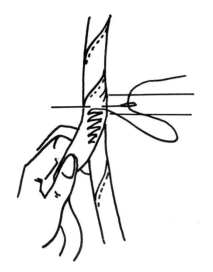

Fig. 19

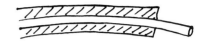

Fig. 20a

Fig. 20b

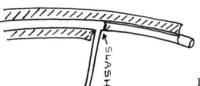

Fig. 20c

Lower Ring. If the struts are to be permanently bound any surplus tape at the end of the strut binding (see page 10) is trimmed off at this stage. Trim it to $\frac{1}{8}''$. The lower ring is then bound as the top ring.

Use of Adhesive Tape. If the shade is to be made exclusively by sticking there is no need to bind the frame with a fabric binding. The fitting may be painted to improve its appearance, but it is not necessary to paint the ring itself, as it is unlikely to be washed.

Method. Carefully unroll a little tape and place the middle of the tape to the inside of the ring (Figure 20a). Taking care not to stretch the tape in case it should split when being rolled over the ring, continue to unroll the tape until the inside of the ring is completely covered and overlap the end by $\frac{1}{2}''$. Roll the bottom edge of the tape up over the ring, slashing it at the junction of the ring and fitting (Figures 20b and c). Finally roll the top edge downwards to complete the preparation.

The join will then be hidden by the cover as it will be on the outside of the ring (see join of tape, page 12). The cover can then be

stuck to this binding by using a clear adhesive very sparingly.

REMEMBER :

(1) After painting the frame, clean the brush with cellulose thinners or turpentine.

(2) If the correct amount of binding has been cut off and this is exhausted before the binding is completed, too much overlapping has occurred. This will produce a thick and bulky ring. Unwind the binding and rebind —do NOT cut off and use a longer piece.

(3) The acute angle of the binding is most important; it prevents the excess overlapping as in para. 2 above.

(4) When binding very large frames the binding may be joined at the junction of any strut with the ring. Finish off a length and rejoin in the usual way. NEVER try to join the binding between struts or the binding will slip back around the ring.

(5) When binding, keep the hands very clean and free from perspiration as the continuous tightening tends to soil the work.

14

3

Materials

MATERIALS which can be used for making lampshades fall mainly into two classes—(a) soft fabrics, and (b) firm materials.

In each class there is a tremendous and ever-increasing range from which to choose. The choice of fabric, as with the style of frame, depends on several factors:

(a) The amount of light required, whether it is transmitted or reflected. The quantity of light available is influenced by the texture and the colour of the cover and the lining materials. Dark colours absorb light, pale colours reflect it and allow light to pass through. For this reason we find that red shades are suitable for television lights, or whenever subdued light is adequate, but a red cover can be used successfully over a white or pastel lining when more light is required. In this case the lining will reflect the light.

(b) The style of the shade to be made. If it is to be pleated, swathed or gathered, the material must drape easily without producing bulk on the rings. Chiffon, georgette and Jap silk (on larger frames) can be used for these styles.

(c) If a shade is deeply bowed (Figure 90) and a tailored cover is to be fitted the material must have plenty of 'give' (see page 26).

(d) If the material is patterned, an interesting motif must be placed centrally in each section. The panel should be large enough to take a complete motif without cutting into it

—the result should be a picture (Plate 13a).

(e) The appearance of the material when the bulb is lighted. Some materials, such as brocades, looked very attractive on an unlit shade but the pattern is completely lost when the light is switched on. These materials are best used on an opaque shade (see pages 18, 19).

(f) The other furnishings in the room and the purpose of the room. Silks, laces, chiffons would not be suitable for a study where a linen-type material or a firm fabric would be much more apt. The colour should pick up some other furnishing in the room, while the texture of the fabric should be in keeping with that of the other furnishings.

(g) The practical qualities of the material. Satins, satinised cotton and glazed chintz reject dust and so keep clean for a longer period than some of the rougher textured fabrics. There are some delightful prints available in glazed chintz. Firm shades of buckram and bonded card cannot be washed.

(h) The texture of the fabric. Embroidered or flock printed fabrics usually have to be fitted on the straight of the material so a suitable frame must be selected. Plate 3 shows a group of wall shades where the Swiss cotton was fitted over Jap silk, the design had to be centralised and the material fitted on the straight of the grain. If these materials are fitted on the cross, bubbles often appear between the motifs of embroidery or the flock printing and these cannot be removed. This is because the embroidery or flock printing affects the uniform stretching of the material. This is another example of the interdependence of frame and material (b and c above).

(i) The time that is available. Shades made of firm material usually take less time than those with covers of soft fabric.

(j) The amount of money that the worker wishes to spend. When making shades with soft covers often good bargains can be found in remnant boxes or during sale-time. Some of the firm fabrics are quite expensive.

(k) The time that the shade is required to last. For example, shades in a nursery, children's room or teenager's room are not expected to last for years. These shades, ideally, should be quickly made, inexpensive and have 'atmosphere', reflecting the interests of the occupant of the room.

SOFT FABRICS

The most successful fabrics are those which have 'give', are strong without being bulky, do not pin-mark and do not easily split or fray.

Some of the most popular include linen, chintz (glazed and unglazed), wild silk, crêpes, shantung and tussore, satinised cotton, gingham, the thinner furnishing fabrics, also many of the materials made from man-made fibres. Some stiff fabrics such as taffeta, and in particular taffeta brocade, are difficult to use as they easily split and the brocade patterns easily break up. Many novelty materials are in the shops today and it is most interesting to experiment with these to obtain unusual and original results.

Chiffon, silk or rayon chiffon and georgette are popular for pleated and swathed shades and they are easy to handle. The texture of chiffon is an aid when pleating as the pleats can follow the texture-lines in the fabric. This is one reason why chiffon should not be ironed before use (see page 46). Nylon chiffon or organza produce very attractive results but these materials do need more care in handling than silk or rayon chiffon. It is not true to say that they are more liable to scorch—this depends on the size of the bulb used compared to the size of the frame (see page 2). As nylon chiffon is so very sheer it is more suitable than silk chiffon when making a cross swathe (Chapter 15). The underlayer of material must be visible through the top layer to give the honeycomb effect.

It has been suggested that some fabrics such as glazed chintz or fabrics made from man-made fibres are not suitable for covering lampshades. To bar these materials would be a great loss to the craft. Some of the most attractive shades incorporate glazed chintz panels (Plates 13a and c). Man-made fibres are used in such a large number of fabrics that it is almost impossible to exclude them from this craft. If, however, the fabric is prone to fray then a suitable seam must be chosen (Chapter 5, page 23).

FIRM FABRICS

Here again the choice is considerable and constantly increasing. Some few years ago there was a very limited choice; parchment, buckram and crinothene were the three firm materials available for making firm shades. Parchment and buckram are still in use but the range of synthetics is greatly increased. There are various forms of acetate, some have fabric ready bonded to them others are attractively textured. In addition there is a wide choice of designs available in fibreglass and parchments.

Apart from the commercially bonded

materials there are two types of parchment to which can be bonded materials of one's own choice. Parbond is an adhesive parchment onto which fabric can be ironed. The parchment is placed with the shiny side uppermost and the fabric placed over it. The heat of the iron melts the adhesive on the card and the fabric adheres to the surface of the card as it cools. Obviously this method cannot be used with pile fabrics such as velvet or with materials containing man-made fibres which would melt before the adhesive. For this reason it is important to test a scrap of the material on a piece of the Parbond before ironing the main portion of the fabric. Fortunately the other type of parchment can be used with these more difficult fabrics. This parchment is known as Selapar and is self-adhesive. When bought it has a protective layer of paper on it which must be peeled away before it can be used. The limitation of Selapar is that it cannot be used as a base for appliqué pieces placed directly on the parchment as the undecorated parts would be sticky. The appliqué must be attached to a background first which is then attached to the Selapar.

Parbond was used as a base for the shade in Plate 14d and Selapar for the shade in Plates 14b, 21c. Wallpaper can be bonded to the Selapar, using spare material left after papering the room in which the shades are to be used. These shades are very inexpensive and very effective.

COLOUR

Obviously colour is a most important factor to consider when selecting the material for any shade. It determines the colour of the light transmitted by the shade and also to a large extent the quantity of light which will pass through the cover. Dark colours absorb light while pale colours reflect it and allow light to pass through. Pink, peach and orange fabrics give a warm light, whereas the light which comes through a green or blue material is much colder.

There is, however, much more tolerance today than in the early days of the craft when cold colours were never used for the covers of shades. Many greens and blues are now used successfully. Maybe the great increase in the number of centrally heated homes is partly responsible for this change; the warmth is there in the home without having to create an illusion of it.

If the colour of the light resulting from a particular fabric is not acceptable, but the material is suitable for other reasons, e.g. linking up various articles of furnishings, the remedy may be to use a lining of a warm tone. Another solution may be to make the shade opaque. An opaque shade is one where very little light actually comes through the cover but it is reflected by a pale lining or in the case of firm materials by the white reverse side of the fabric. In soft-fabric shades the opaqueness may be achieved by inserting a dark interlining.

Experimenting with colour can give very rewarding results but always test the material, together with any lining which is to be used, over a light before making up the shade. Far too much work goes into a lampshade to risk failure when a simple test can forecast the amount and tone of the light to be expected from the finished article.

4

Linings [Plate 1]

LININGS PLAY a very important part in many shades. They may be used for a variety of reasons and they can vary in type and method of construction.

FUNCTIONS OF A LINING

1. A lining can be used to hide the struts. Many people dislike seeing the struts in a completed shade. In an unlined shade they appear as hard lines breaking the smoothness of the fabric even though they have been painted or bound to match the cover fabric. They are particularly obvious in hanging shades where the inside of the shade is very noticeable; these struts can be hidden by a lining placed inside the frame.

2. It can give substance to a cover when a thin or open fabric such as chiffon or lace is being used for the top cover; it should not be possible to discern the outline of the bulb through the cover.

3. A lining can be used to alter the colour of the light transmitted through a particular cover. A pink lining can change the colour of a sickly yellow light or a cold white light to a warm glow.

4. A pale-coloured or white lining will increase the amount of reflected light. Plate 1e shows a wide but shallow drum which has a dark red pleated cover with a white lining and it is used successfully in a hall.

TYPES OF LININGS

A. *Balloon Lining or Internal Lining.* Plate 1d. This is a lining which is fitted inside the frame to hide the struts (see para. 1 above). It is tailored so that it has no fullness. Usually it is made from two sections but in some shades, e.g. the square bowed shade (Chapter 8, Plate 13a), the lining is composed of four panels.

B. *External Lining* (Plates 1a, f, g). This is really an under-cover, attached outside the struts. It is fitted and assembled exactly as a cover. It is used when a lining is needed to give substance to a top cover (see para. 2 above), or to alter the tone of the transmitted light (see para. 3). On small candle shades it is impossible to use an internal lining as it would be too close to the bulb and so scorch or burn—hence if a lining is necessary an external one is used. In this case the struts would be painted or bound to match the lining (Plates 1 and 3).

C. *A combination of both A and B.* These two linings may then fulfil functions 1, 2, and 4, above, as in : —

(i) A pleated shade with a dark cover of touching pleats and a pale internal lining is usually improved by a dark interlining. This prevents any hair-line cracks between pleats being visible when the bulb is lighted.

(ii) If the material of the cover loses its beauty, as do some brocades, when the bulb is lighted a dark interlining can be used. This makes the shade opaque and the effective light is that reflected by the lining. The cover then remains attractive at all times.

D. *Pleated Internal Lining*. Spaced pleating produces an interesting result in a wide drum shade (Plate 1e). For this type of lining allow twice the circumference of the bottom ring × the height of the drum.

E. *A Semi-pleated or Gathered Lining*. Here the lining is a straight piece of material. In size it measures the circumference of the frame × the depth of the shade. This type of lining can be used successfully in a collared empire frame (Figures 5c and 80) or a scalloped drum (Figure 77 and Plate 13b).

F. *Decorative Lining*. This is really a variation of a balloon lining but made of the cover material. It is most successful in a coolie shade. Here the lining is more in view than the cover and so the lining material is more important than the actual cover. In Plates 4 and 5 the coolie shades have the cover and the lining made of the same fabric.

TYPES OF MATERIALS FOR LINING

It is important that the material chosen should be strong but supple and there is a wide range of fabrics from which to choose. The material should not pin-mark, nor should it split easily, so taffeta is a bad choice.

Crêpe-backed satin, tussore, shantung, Jap silk, Taiho, tricel and lawn can all be used with success depending on the shade being made. The crêpe-backed satin is probably the most useful of all the fabrics; it is extremely supple, it can be used with the satin side inside to reflect the maximum amount of light or it can be used under a thin or open material with the satin side shining through to give a very rich effect.

Jap silk is ideal if two linings are to be fitted as with some pleated or gathered shades. Plates 19a and b.

When deciding the colour of the lining, it should always be tested under the cover fabric over a lighted lamp. The shade with the tie-dye cover (Plate 15c) has a blue lining. any other colour completely destroyed the effect of the design when it was over a light. Pink, rust or peach linings give a warm light while cream or white linings reflect the maximum amount of light.

Linings are inserted before the cover is attached in the majority of shades where the cover is not pleated, swathed or gathered, as neatening is easier when the work is done in this order (see pages 32–34). An exception to this rule is made when the cover fabric is very firm and has little 'give'. Here as with pleating, etc., the tightening of the cover would cause the lining to lose its tautness and ruin the final effect.

CUTTING LININGS

Tailored linings may be fitted on the straight or on the cross of the grain (see Chapter 6). When internal or balloon linings which have been cut on the cross are inserted they bow away from the struts (Figure 21). This is a disadvantage in small shades as the material will be very close to the bulb and therefore will scorch. However, in a standard shade the effect of the bowing is very pleasing. These shades are usually quite high and the lining is visible and the curve formed by the lining ballooning away from the frame gives a good line.

Linings fitted on the straight of the grain hang much closer to the struts and hence are preferable for small shades. They also use slightly less material.

Fig. 21 Lining on the cross bowing away from the frame

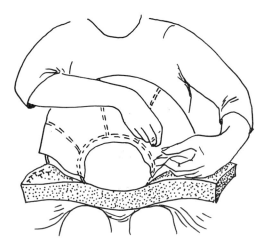

Fig. 22 To show method of working with protective pad of plastic foam on the knees

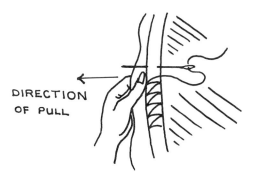

DIRECTION
OF PULL

Fig. 23a

Fig. 23b

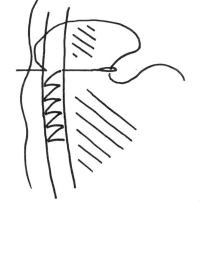

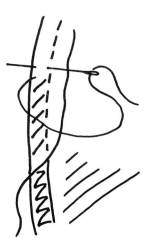

Fig. 24

5

Techniques

PINNING

IN THE making of soft-fabric shades this is a very important technique. The fabric is pinned to the bound frame in order to fit a section of the cover or lining. This is either preparatory to stitching directly to the frame as in a panelled shade (Chapter 8), or marking it before removing the section for assembly as for the tailored shades (Chapter 6). Accuracy and tautness are essential.

It is important that the correct pins (Lills) are used (see page 6) and that they are correctly inserted. They should be placed horizontally through the material and pass through the binding on the frame. They should be inserted with the direction of the strain or tightening, i.e., the point should be away from the centre of the panel (Figure 36). If the point faces inwards when the pin is inserted, the pressure is against the tightening of the fabric and it is more difficult to obtain a really taut panel. It is also easier to remove a pin pointing outwards when stitching—the left hand holds the raw edge and the needle hand can remove the pin without losing any tautness (Figure 23a). For a left-handed worker the reverse order would operate. In no case should the pins pass underneath the struts or the rings.

Woollen or jersey clothing is not ideal garb when pinning lampshades as the pins catch in the clothing and can be pulled out of position. A piece of 1″ polyether or plastic foam makes an ideal cushion on the knee. It protects both the worker and the lampshade, does not catch onto the pins and incidentally acts as a pincushion (Figure 22). Once pins become blunted or bent they should be thrown away.

STITCHING

(a) *To attach covers or linings to the frame*. The most effective stitch is a two-stage stitch, often known—particularly by glove makers—as Streetly Stitch.

For right-handed workers: holding the raw edge of the material with the left hand and tightening if necessary (see above) insert the needle through the material and the binding (Figure 23a). Draw the needle through and reinsert in exactly the same place (Figure 23b). Then pick up the fabric and the binding $\frac{1}{8}$″ further on and repeat the stitch (Figure 23a). This gives a 'Z' shaped stitch which is both strong and neat.

Never use a long length of thread as it will break before it is fully used and also it will become entangled around the pins.

(b) *To neaten the raw edges of the cover*. Roll back the surplus material onto the cover —do not pull it back or the cover may be slackened. Work single stitches about $\frac{1}{4}$″

apart making sure that the stitches do not break the rolled edge as this may be visible (particularly at the bottom ring), after the trimming has been attached (Figure 24).

Only a small amount of material should be picked up for the stitch especially on small shades. The bigger the stitch, the wider the trimming necessary to cover the stitches and the raw edge. Trim very close to the stitches.

(c) *To stitch firm materials to rings.* Many of these materials are very liable to tear and so great care is needed when stitching. The minimum of strain should be placed on the material and this can be achieved by stitching into the binding of the ring through the fabric (Figure 25a). In this case the material is pressed onto the ring. If the stitch passes through the ring and out through material this will tend to tear away at the previous stitch (Figure 25b).

The thread passes over the edge of the material and so is an oversewing stitch but these stitches are hidden by the trimming.

If the material is tough a running stitch can be used. The needle is passed through the material into the binding at an angle. It is then reinserted, again at an angle and only a fraction of an inch from where it came out. The thread is caught for a length in the binding without being visible. The space between the stitches should be about $\frac{1}{2}''$ (Figure 26).

(d) *To attach braids, fringes, etc.* Here there is very little strain on the stitch and so they can be comparatively large. A variation of herringbone stitch is successful, but the longer sections of the stitch are hidden.

Bring the needle through the trimming near one edge. Reinsert a small way behind where the thread came out pointing the needle towards the opposite edge of the trimming and at an acute angle. Repeat the stitch going back to the first edge of the trimming. As the thread is tightened the stitch be-

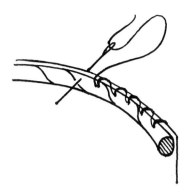

Fig. 25a Correct method

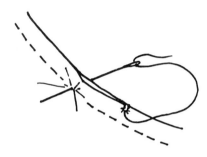

Fig. 25b Incorrect method—tearing material

Fig. 26

22

comes almost or even completely invisible depending on the texture of the trimming (Figures 27a and b).

(e) *Stitching the seams.* For lined shades a single seam is usually the best choice unless the material is very liable to fray. If a swing-needle machine is available this can be used to prevent fraying on a single seam. On bowed shades, in particular, it is advisable to avoid a French seam or even double machining, as these tend to prevent the seam allowance stretching where it passes over the curve. When making an unlined shade, if a swing-needle machine is not available a French seam has to be used; in this case it must be kept very narrow, no wider than the strut of the frame over which it is to sit.

The size of the machine-stitch used should be carefully selected and tested on a scrap of the fabric being used. If the stitch is too large it will be very obvious when the cover is placed over the frame. When the material is tightened against the seam (Figure 28a) gaps will appear between the stitches (Figure 28b).

If the stitch used is too large the seam will also be much more liable to crack under the strain when the cover is being fitted. If a swing-needle machine is used a slight zig-zag stitch will give a more elastic seam, but

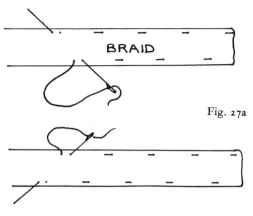

Fig. 27a

Fig. 27b

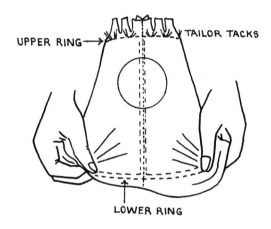

Fig. 28a

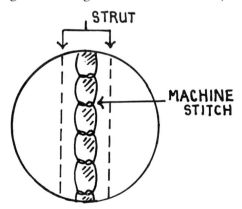

Fig. 28b Enlargement of seam showing the effect of having too large a stitch

again the size of the stitch must be carefully adjusted. At any setting the stitch appears twice as large when used as a zig-zag as when used for straight stitching (Figure 29).

TAILOR TACKS

After a tailored lining or cover has been pinned onto the frame the fitting line is marked along both struts and the top ring with a pencil. After the lining or cover has been assembled and is ready for attaching to the frame it will be found that the position of the top ring line is marked on one piece of fabric but not on the other—this marking is

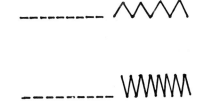

Fig. 29 Changing from straight stitch to zig-zag doubles the effective size of the stitch

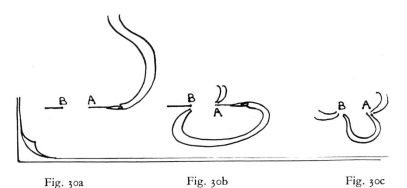

Fig. 30a   Fig. 30b   Fig. 30c

now transferred by means of tailor's tacks. These are looped tacking stitches with a back stitch.

To Work

(1) With a long piece of double cotton pick up $\frac{1}{2}''$ of material at one end of the marked line going into the fabric at A and out at B (Figure 30a).

(2) Pick up the same piece of material again, in at A and out at B (Figure 30b).

(3) Draw the needle through but do not tighten completely; leave a loop (Figure 30c).

(4) Move forward 1″ and work another stitch. Repeat this along the whole line.

(5) Snip between the separate tacks so that each looks like the stitch in Figure 30c.

(6) Slide the hand between the two pieces of material, snip the threads between the two layers leaving loose ends in both.

NEATENERS

These are used to neaten any raw or frayed edges where the lining has been slashed at the junction of the fitting and the ring. They are made from crossway strips of fabric cut 1″–1$\frac{1}{2}$″ wide. The two long edges are folded inwards almost to meet (1st fold), and then the strip is folded in half (Figure 31). This

24

strip is then tacked. The first folds can be pressed with an iron, but if the second fold is not pressed the resulting rolled effect is most pleasing.

To use: These neateners are inserted after the lining has been fitted, whether it has been inserted before or after the cover (Chapter 6). Place one strip round the fitting so that a V fold is formed (Figure 32). Do not pull it up tight around the fitting. Place the two ends side by side—do not overlap them as this produces bulk on the ring. Secure with the stitch (Figures 23a and b). Trim off any surplus material from the neatener and draw out the tacking thread (see above).

REMEMBER

(1) The frame is comparatively delicate so handle it with care.

(2) When picking up a shade always do so by the fitting, NEVER by the body of the shade or the tautness will be lost.

(3) With so many pins employed pin pricks are an obvious risk. If bleeding occurs stop work immediately until the flow has ceased. If blood spots the material moisten a length of sewing cotton with warm water and wind it round a finger. Work it in a circular motion over the stain. If the mark occurs before the fabric is stitched to the frame it is often better to wash the section of material in a little warm water as many fabrics ring mark with moisture.

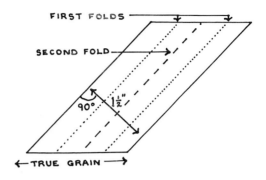

Fig. 31

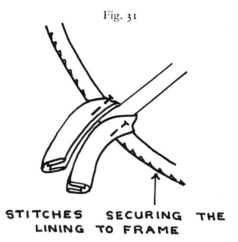

STITCHES SECURING THE LINING TO FRAME

Fig. 32

6

Tailored Covers and Linings [Plates 2A, 2B & 5]

'TAILORED' is the term usually applied to those covers or linings which fit onto the frame with no fullness and where the joins of the two or more sections are such that they require no trimming to neaten any raw edges. These joins are either single or French seams and they usually, but not always, sit over a strut. Exceptions are the linings of the shades in Plate 11. When a seam sits on a strut it must sit exactly over the strut and have a perfectly smooth line. Achieving this is one of the important skills of the craft.

It will be found that when selecting a frame for an Empire shade which is to have a tailored cover it must have at least six struts. Some Empire frames have two rings joined by only four struts. If such a frame is fitted with a tailored cover the result is very ugly, the shade is round at the top and bottom and square in the middle.

ON THE CROSS OR ON THE STRAIGHT?

This can be a very vexed subject, but both methods have their advantages. In fact there are occasions when one or the other method is the only one which will give a satisfactory result. The correct method is the one which will give the best result for (a) the shape of the frame, and (b) the texture and the pattern of the material used for that particular shade.

Examples

(1) For bowed empire shades—either method can be used if the fabric has plenty of give and the design is suitable. The linings produced by the two methods will fit differently to the frame (see Linings, page 19).

(2) A bowed drum MUST have the cover fitted on the cross so that the middle of the cover, which is narrow, will stretch to pass over the top ring (Figure 33).

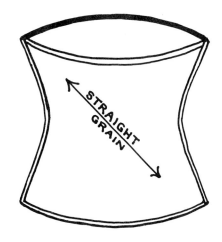

Fig. 33

(3) Bowed empire shades, where the fabric chosen for the cover is very stiff or has little give, must have the cover fitted on the cross so that the bubble which appears in the centre of the half-section can be removed by stretching.

26

(4) On bowed or straight empire shades striped material must be fitted on the straight of the fabric. Checked material may be fitted on the cross, in which case the checks must be matched at the seams (Figure 34).

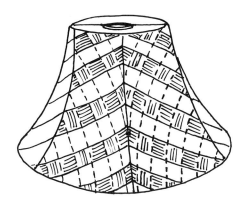

Fig. 34

(5) Straight-sided drums must have their covers and linings fitted on the straight of the fabric in order to keep the shape of the frame (Figure 60, on page 43).

METHOD OF FITTING ON THE CROSS—*Lining or Cover*

This method is probably the easier for a complete novice as any slight inaccuracy can usually be eliminated when the lining or cover is being fitted to the frame because it is on the cross.

Prepare the frame by painting and binding; two opposite struts must be bound (see page 10). The binding on these two struts may be removed before the lining or the cover is attached. Iron the material.

The cover or lining will be in two sections—hence one section is fitted to half the frame.

1. Lie the frame on its side, with the two bound struts as in Figure 35. With the wrong side of the material uppermost, place the material over the frame so the true cross runs from the centre of the top ring to the centre of the bottom ring (Figure 35). Place four temporary pins at the top and the bottom of each bound strut, i.e. at A, B, C and D. These pins can be glass-headed. If the material is patterned, an interesting motif should be in the centre of the panel.

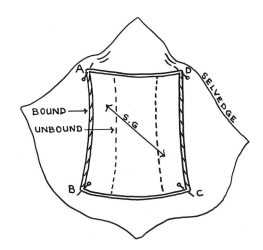

Fig. 35

2. Pin every half inch down the left-hand strut, AB, just taking out any obvious fullness near the strut (Figures 36a and b).

3. Return to the top of the left-hand strut, i.e. point A. From this point follow the grain of the fabric until it strikes either the bottom ring (Figure 36b) or the opposite strut (Figure 36a) at point X. The exact spot will depend on the shape and height of the frame. Tighten along this line AX and pin. Continue pinning from X to B, always tightening along the grain and away from the strut AB (Figures 36a and b).

N.B. Some wrinkles may appear but these will be removed later (see page 28).

4. Tightening along the grain from strut

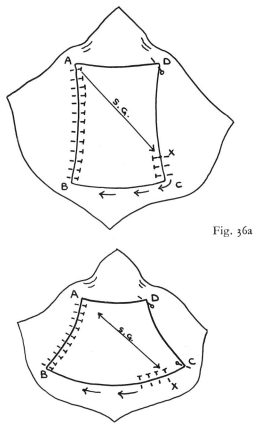

Fig. 36a

Fig. 36b

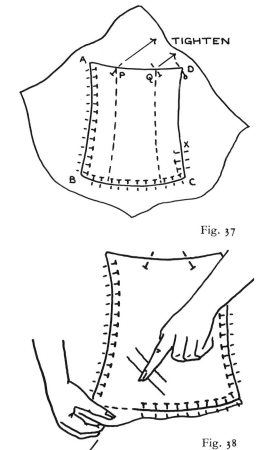

Fig. 37

Fig. 38

PULL

AB, put in a pin at the top of the second strut (P) and at the top of the third strut (Q).

5. Remove the temporary pin at D and tighten the fabric again pulling along the grain and replace the pin at D (Figure 37).

6. Complete the pinning along the lower edge; i.e. from X to C if necessary (see para. 3 above).

7. Tightening along the grain of the fabric complete the pinning of the half-section, i.e. of the strut DC working from D to C or D to X.

N.B. If any wrinkles remain in the material they may be removed by placing a

finger across them and at right angles to them, then tightening in the direction indicated by the fingernail. It will of course be necessary to take out several pins (Figure 38).

8. Using Tailor's chalk or a pencil, mark VERY LIGHTLY along the pinning on both struts and the top ring, not along the bottom ring except for half an inch at each end, i.e. B and C.

Trim off any surplus material at the bottom edge $1''–1\frac{1}{2}''$ below the ring.

N.B. With a petal-edge frame do not cut

28

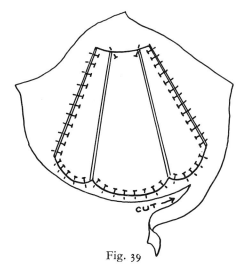

Fig. 39

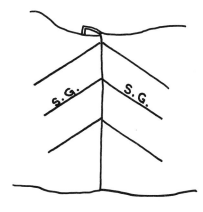

Fig. 41a Showing the grain of both sections meeting the seam at the same angle

up into scallops but in a straight line $1''-1\frac{1}{2}''$ below the bottom of the scallops (Figure 39). Remove all pins.

To Assemble—Lining and Cover

9. With the right sides of the fabric together place the marked panel onto the remainder of the material, making sure that the grain matches EXACTLY (Figure 40). Failure to ensure this can cause difficulty later; when inserting the lining. Tiny puckers

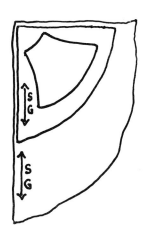

Fig. 40

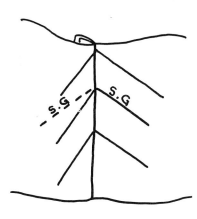

Fig. 41b Showing the grain of one section meeting the seam at a very acute angle: dotted line would be correct

may appear which cannot be eradicated—this is due to the fact that the threads of the two sections meet the seam at different angles (Figures 41a and b).

10. Pin along the strut lines and tack just outside these. Machine-stitch on the pencil lines commencing $1''$ before the line of the top ring (i.e. at A) and continuing $1''$ below

29

the line of the bottom ring (i.e. at B) (Figure 42).

11. Tailor tack along the line of the top ring (i.e. A to D) to mark where the material will fit to the top ring on the second half of the cover or lining (Figure 43). Snip through the tailor tacks.

12. Trim the side seams to $\frac{1}{8}''$ and the top

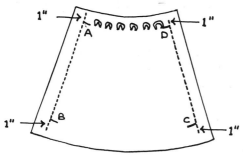

Fig. 42

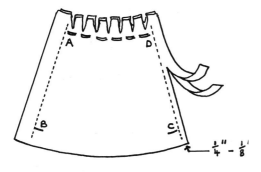

Fig. 43

edge to 1″. Slash inwards for $\frac{1}{2}''$–1″ along the top edge (Figure 43). This will allow the material to roll over the ring during fitting (Figure 48).

METHOD OF FITTING ON THE STRAIGHT—Linings or Covers (Not Drum Frames)

Prepare the frame: paint it, bind both rings and two opposite struts. Iron the material and place wrong side uppermost.

1. Place the frame on its side and lie the material over it so that the grain runs exactly from the centre of the top ring (M) to the centre of the bottom ring (N). Pin at these points but do NOT tighten between them; the material should fit to the frame and not jump off it (Figure 44).

2. Pin the material to the bound strut (AB) at the mid-point X. Tighten across the frame

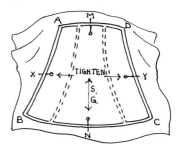

Fig. 44

to the middle of the opposite strut and pin at point Y (Figure 44).

3. Working away from these two points pin upwards towards the top ring and downwards towards the lower ring, tightening always in the direction shown by the arrows in Figure 45 below. Work first on one strut

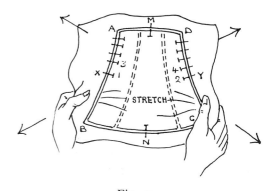

Fig. 45

and then on the other as suggested by the numbered pins (Figure 45).

N.B. A. It is important to check constantly that the grain runs in a straight line from M to N.

B. When the sides are completely pinned the material should be very tight. On bowed frames horizontal wrinkles will almost certainly have appeared (Figure 46). These will be removed during the next stage.

4. Tighten the material vertically (i.e. between the rings) just sufficiently to remove any wrinkles. Pin along both rings (Figure 46). On bowed frames overtightening at this stage causes loss of shape as the material jumps from ring to ring rather than follows the curved line of the strut. This is a very common fault on shades where the cover has been fitted on the straight.

5. Mark very lightly the pin-line along both struts, the top ring and $\frac{1}{2}''$ in from the ends of the struts along the bottom ring.

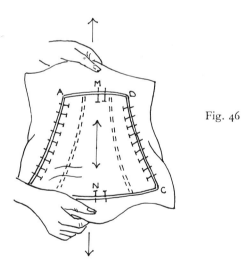

Fig. 46

Trim away any surplus material to $1''$ all round the shade. Remove the pins.

To Assemble

6. With the right sides of the materials together, place the marked panel onto the rest

of the fabric, matching the grain exactly (see paragraph 9, page 29).

When assembling either a lining or a cover cut on the cross the machining is done ON the marked line in both cases. Because the material IS cut on the cross it can be pulled to fit even when the lining goes inside the frame; in this respect it is an easy method. When the lining is cut on the straight this is impossible and so it must be made to fit exactly. No fullness can be eradicated after the seams have been machined, hence the lining must be tested for fit between the tacking and machining stages.

Lining

7a. Using the materials prepared in stage 6, pin these together placing the pins on the pencilled line. Draw a second line about $\frac{1}{8}''$ $-\frac{1}{4}''$ in from the original line at points A and B, also at C and D, but curving in at the centre to $\frac{3}{8}''-\frac{1}{2}''$ from the original line (Figure 47). The larger frames, of thicker wire, need the greater reduction. Using quite small stitches tack along the new lines ready for testing. Tailor tack along the top ring line and slash

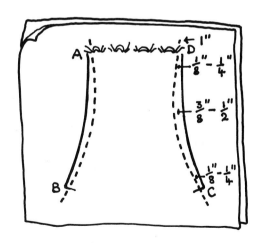

Fig. 47

to within $\frac{1}{2}''$ of this line. Snip through the tailor tacks.

8a. Place the lining inside the frame and pin the material to the top and bottom of the struts AB and CD. Turn the spare $1''$ at the top into the shade so that it is not bunched around the fitting. Fit it to the tops of the other struts; it should appear quite tight. Repeat over the lower ring.

If the lining appears to fit very easily or is obviously too large, retack, increasing the seam allowance. If the lining is too tight—so that it may split or will not roll over the rings—retack outside the first tacking. When the fit is satisfactory machine the seams on the tacking lines and trim the seams to $\frac{1}{8}''$.

Extend the machining $1''$ at the top and bottom of each seam (See Figure 42).

Cover

7b. Pin and tack the two sections together keeping the tacking stitches just outside of the pencil line.

8b. Machine the two sections together, stitching ON the pencil line and extending the stitching $1''$ beyond the ring line at each end (Figure 42). Trim away the surplus material from the side seams to $\frac{1}{8}''$.

COVERS FOR UNLINED SHADES

These are fitted exactly as for lined shades up to paragraph 8, page 28 (for shades on the cross) or paragraph 6, page 31 (for shades on the straight) except that the material is placed over the frame RIGHT SIDE uppermost.

Proceed now as follows:

1. With the WRONG sides of the materials together place the marked panel over the rest of the material, matching the grain exactly (see paragraph 9, page 29).

2. Tack the two materials together stitching on the pencil line.

3. Machine $\frac{1}{8}''$ outside the tacking line and trim to just less than $\frac{1}{8}''$. Press the seam open, turn the cover with the wrong side outside and complete the French seam.

TO INSERT THE LINING

In tailored shades it is usual to insert the lining before attaching the cover. If the work is done in this order it is easier to neaten the stitching on the rings (see page 33, paragraph 6). However, there are occasions when it is necessary to reverse the order. If the cover fabric is very stiff, with very little 'give' and a bowed frame is being used considerable strain may be placed on the frame while getting the cover sufficiently tight. If the lining is inserted first in this case it may lose its tautness during the tightening of the cover, so it should be inserted after the cover has been attached.

Method

Remove the binding from the two struts. Iron the lining but do not open out the seam.

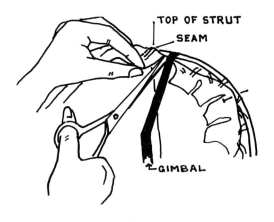

Fig. 48

32

1. Put the lining inside the frame so that the seams will fit to those struts nearest to where the fittings join the ring (Figure 48). Pin at A, B, C, and D.

2. Roll back the surplus material at the top inside the ring, and at the junction of the fitting and the ring, slash up to the tailor's tack and $\frac{1}{8}''$ beyond (Figure 48). It may be necessary to increase this slash slightly later during the fitting.

3. Now roll the surplus material over the ring and pin at the top of each strut and about every $1''$–$1\frac{1}{2}''$ between the struts. At this stage the tailor tacks should be on the ring.

4. Stand the frame on its top ring with one seam away from the body. Using both hands, one each side of the seam, tighten the material over the bottom ring (Figure 49). The tightening should be along the line of the grain. The seam should not be pulled out

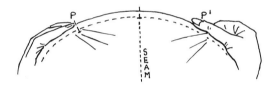

Fig. 49

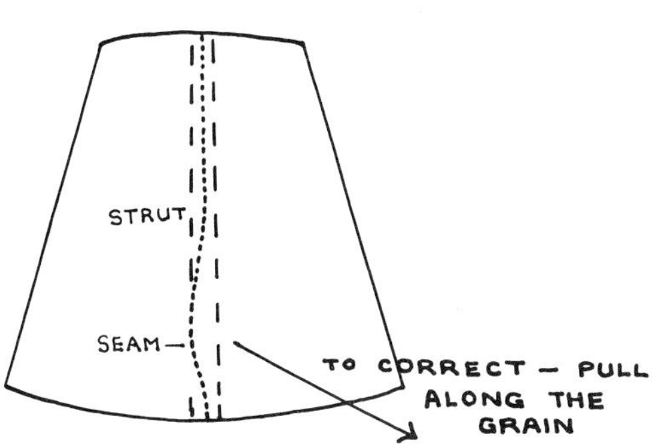

STRUT

SEAM

TO CORRECT — PULL ALONG THE GRAIN

Fig. 50

of its line over the strut (Figure 50). When correct, release one side holding the other side firmly and pin at P. The seam will go off strut temporarily but will be corrected when the material is retightened and the pin inserted at P^1. Turn the frame round and fit each side of the other seam. Continue to fit working against each seam alternately until the lining appears quite tight.

5. Retighten along the top ring if necessary. If a few obstinate wrinkles remain, remove these by tightening at right angles to them (page 28, para. 7, Figure 38).

6. When the lining is tight and wrinkle free, stitch on the outside of the rings using the stitch shown in Figures 23a and b. If the stitching is on the outside of the ring it will be hidden when the cover is fitted over it.

Trim away any surplus material to $\frac{1}{8}''$. If the material is liable to fray overcast the raw edge.

Neateners. Make the neateners (Figures 31, 32) and attach these to neaten the slashes made where the fitting joins the ring. Stitch them to the outside of the ring and trim off any surplus, or this will show when the bulb is lit.

TO ATTACH THE COVER

1. Place the cover over the frame so that the seams of the cover are over those of the lining.

2. Slide the cover down until the tailor tacking marking the position of the top ring is in position over the ring. Pin at the top of each strut, and then every inch around this ring.

3. Pin the lower points of the seam, i.e. points B and C, to the bottom of the respective struts.

4. Working outwards from the seams, first on one side and then the other and tighten-

ing along the grain of the cover fabric pin along the bottom edge. Any wrinkles can be removed by tightening at right angles to them (see Figure 38).

5. Stitch along the BOTTOM of the ring thus obscuring the stitches anchoring the lining (see paragraph 6, page 33). Stitch the top ring in a similar way.

6. Roll back the surplus material on each ring and catch back with the single stitch (Figure 24).

7. Trim away any surplus material right back to the neatening stitches. The shade is now ready for the trimming to be attached, —this will cover the last row of stitches and the raw edges.

N.B. Do make sure that there are no loose tacking threads, untrimmed or frayed edges left between the lining and the cover or these will ruin the shade; they appear as shadows when a light is under the shade.

N.B. If the cover has to be attached before the lining this is done exactly as above (paras. 1–5). The surplus material is trimmed right back to the stitches. The lining is then inserted and it is most important that the stitches anchoring it to the frame are on the OUTSIDE of the rings so that they will be covered by the trimming. They must also be very small and close together. If the lining

material is liable to fray the raw edge may be overcast after trimming.

Suggested Quantities
Fitted on the Cross of the Material.

10″ Bowed Empire, height 7″: $\frac{1}{3}$yd. 36″ material.

12″–14″ shade, height 8″–9″: $\frac{1}{2}$yd. 36″ material.

20″ shade, height 13″ approx.: 1yd. 36″ material.

24″ shade, height 14″ approx.: $1\frac{1}{4}$yd. 36″ material.

10″ Bowed Drum, height 7″: $\frac{1}{2}$yd. 36″ material.

12″ Bowed Drum, height 10″: $\frac{3}{4}$yd. 36″ material.

Fitted on the Straight of the material.

10″–12″ Bowed Empire: $\frac{1}{3}$yd.

14″ shade: $\frac{1}{2}$yd.

20″ shade: $\frac{3}{4}$yd.

Chimney Bowed Empire (Plate 15b), Diameter 14″, height 18″: $\frac{5}{8}$yd.

Coolie shade (Plate 4b). Diameter 12″, height 5″: $\frac{1}{2}$yd for lining and cover.

Candle shade. Diameter 5″, height 4″: 2 shades from $\frac{1}{6}$yd.

Candle shade. Diameter 6″, height $4\frac{1}{2}$″ 2 shades from $\frac{1}{4}$yd.

7

Shades with Openwork Covers [Plate 4b]

WHEN ANY material such as lace, broderie anglaise, pulled or drawn linen embroidery is chosen for the top cover of a shade, an external lining (see page 18) must be used. Without this lining the struts would be visible through the mesh of the top cover. The shade may then have an internal or balloon lining in addition—this is a matter of choice. If an internal lining is not used the struts must be painted or bound to match the external lining (see page 9).

The major problem when using an openwork fabric for the lampshade cover is to prevent fraying ends or fabric appearing through the openwork at the seams.* The problem may be overcome in various ways.

The outer, openwork cover and the external lining may be made up and attached separately or they may be put together and treated as one fabric. Much depends on the shape of the frame, the texture of the outer cover, the type of machine being used and whether the lining and the lace are the same colour.

If a swing-needle machine is available and if the cover and the lace are the same colour, then the two materials may be made up separately using a small stitch and a narrow ziz-zag. Both seams are trimmed back to the stitches and no raw edges will appear through

* For ease of description the openwork fabric will be referred to as lace.

the lace. As the seams are automatically neatened with the zig-zag the seam of the lining can face to the inside of the shade and will be hidden by the strut. If the lining is a darker colour than the lace there will be a hard line of light coloured stitching visible down the seam.

The great advantage of making the two materials up as one is that no raw edges will show through the open mesh of the outer cover. Moreover, there will be neither the problem of matching the seams of the two covers, nor will there be a hard line of machine-stitching visible along the line of the seam. On drum frames there are no problems in working the two fabrics together and the number of operations in making up the shade is halved. With some bowed frames, however, more care is needed. If the lace is very soft and has a great deal of elasticity it is more difficult to tighten the combined cover without drawing the lace up off the lining; extra care is needed during fitting (see paragraph 3 below).

TO MAKE UP A COVER AS ONE MATERIAL

(*No inner lining*)

1. Fold the lining material in half—the right sides together.
2. Fold the lace in half with the right

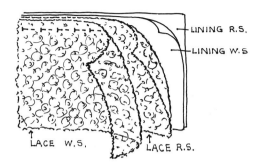

Fig. 51a

sides together and place over the folded lining (Figure 51a). Pin or tack the four layers of material together along the top edge —not down the sides.

3. Using the four layers of materials as one and with the lining material to the frame fit as for a tailored shade on the straight. (See pages 30–31 for empire shade or pages 43–44 for drum shades). GREAT CARE must be taken that all the layers are tight. It will probably be found that the lace will stretch more than the lining and this should be done to avoid difficulties during the refitting of the cover. When this refitting is complete the lace should sit on the lining and not stand off it at all.

4. When the pinning is done mark the fitting line—not with pencil—but with a tacking thread. Care must be taken not to stitch to the binding of the frame, although the tacking must go through all four layers of material. Pencil marking is inadequate on openwork fabrics as it will only soil the lace and it will not hold the layers together—which is most important. These layers must not be allowed to move before they have been tacked together. This is on account of the different degrees of elasticity of the lace and the lining. After tacking remove the pins.

5. Machine the layers together—the stit-

ches being $\frac{1}{8}''$ outside the tacking line. Trim the lace back to just outside the machining and the lining to slightly less than $\frac{1}{8}''$.

6. Turn the bottom layer of the lining over the rest of the cover (the lace will now be sandwiched between the two pieces of lining (Figure 51b). Tack the seam flat.

7. Complete the French seam by machining $\frac{1}{8}''$ in from the folded edge; this row of stitching should be on the original tacking line (paragraph 4). Remove all tackings except those along the top ring line. Tailor tack along this line and snip these tackings.

8. Turn the cover so that the lace is on the outside. All the raw edges will be hidden.

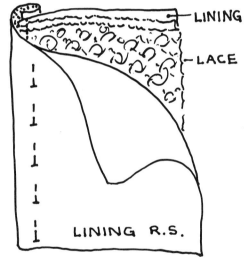

Fig. 51b

9. Fit this cover onto the frame as described on pages 33–34 or 45, taking care to tighten both layers of the cover so that there are no wrinkles in either when the stitching to the frame begins.

10. Stitch to the top or bottom of the two rings. To avoid bulk on the rings trim the lace right back to the stitches and roll back the lining to neaten (Figure 24).

36

TO MAKE UP A COVER AS ONE MATERIAL

(Inner or balloon lining to be used)

1. Fit and assemble the internal lining as in Chapter 6 or Chapter 10.

2. Tear the material for the external lining in half. Fold the lace in half with the right sides together.

3. Place the folded lace to the wrong side of one half of the lining. Pin or tack these three layers together along the top edge. N.B. At this stage the materials will be as Figure 51 without the bottom layer of the lining.

4. Fit and mark as for the previous cover (page 36, paragraphs 3 and 4) but with the three layers of fabric instead of four. It is always necessary, in view of its greater elasticity, to work with the lace uppermost and so to ensure that it is quite tight when fitted.

5. Place the remaining half of the lining over the lace, with the wrong side of the lining to the wrong side of the lace. Tack together on the fitting line, i.e. on top of the tackings from paragraph 4. Machine the side seams just inside but as close as possible to the tacking. After stitching remove all the tackings on the seams and trim the seams to $\frac{1}{8}''$. Tailor tack the line of the top ring and turn the cover.

N.B. A French seam is not needed with an internal lining. Complete the shade as for a lined shade (see Chapter 6). Again trim away the lace before neatening the external lining (see paragraph 10 above).

8

Sectional or Panelled Shades [Plate 13a]

THESE SHADES are both very useful and very interesting to make. They enable one to combine two materials and this can be used to highlight attractive motifs or to pick out and emphasise a chosen colour (Plate 13a). These particular shades illustrate how glazed chintz can be used very successfully (see page 15). These shades also illustrate the importance of planning a balance between the amount of pattern and the amount of plain material which will give the most pleasing result. If four patterned panels had been used in shade 13a there would have been too much pattern and the impact of the design would have been lost. Shade 13c shows how the same effect can be achieved by changing one of the materials; in this case chiffon replaces the wild silk of shade 13a. These two shades team well and yet have that extra interest which would not have been achieved had exactly the same materials been used for both shades. Both the wild silk and the chiffon pick up the sage green in the bird panels.

BOWED SQUARE DRUM (Plate 13a)

Prepare the frame: If the shade is to be lined bind the struts with $\frac{1}{4}''$ tape (page 10, paragraphs 1–4) and both rings with $\frac{3}{8}''$ tape. If the shade is to be unlined bind the struts with matching ribbon, or strips of self material (page 10).

Lining

This shade is not easily lined by any of the previously described methods but the following method is both successful and quite easy to do.

1. Place a rectangle of lining fabric over one panel of the frame—right side uppermost. Pin at the mid-points, X and Y, of the struts AB and CD and tighten between these two points. X–Y must be on the true grain of the material (Figure 52).

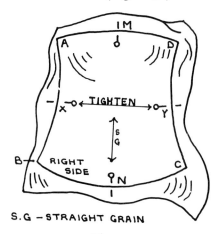

Fig. 52

2. Working from X and Y, pin firstly upwards to the top ring and then down towards the bottom ring, tightening between the two struts. Horizontal wrinkles will appear but these will be removed later (Figure 53).

3. Pin along the top and bottom edges,

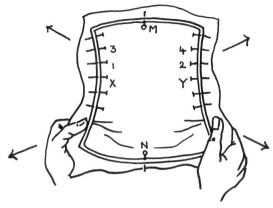

Fig. 53

AD and BC, of the panel, tightening just sufficiently to remove the wrinkles and to get a smooth curve along the rings (Figure 54).

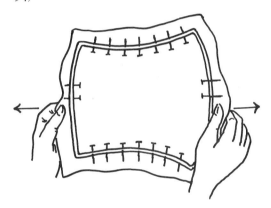

Fig. 54

4. With a sharp pencil or tailor's chalk and working from the inside of the frame, mark around the inside of the struts and rings (Figure 55); this will be on the wrong side of the material.

5. Trim the surplus material away; to $\frac{1}{2}''$ outside each strut and to $1''-1\frac{1}{2}''$ outside the top and bottom rings. Remove the pins.

6. Check if the four panels are identical. If they are not, each panel must be fitted and marked individually. Distinctive marks must be made on both the frame and the panel to ensure that each is refitted to the correct panel. If the panels are identical a template can be made from the first panel. Place the panel over a piece of paper with the pencil marking uppermost. Using a tracing wheel mark along the pencilling (Figure 56). Cut along the perforations on the paper. With this template mark out three more lining sections (Figure 57).

7. To assemble the lining, pin D1 to A2,

Fig. 55

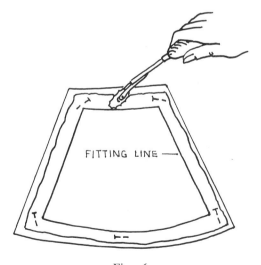

Fig. 56

39

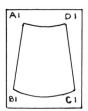 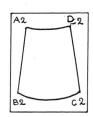 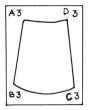 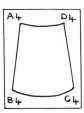

Fig. 57

and C1 to B2;—D2 to A3, and C2 to B3 and so to join the four sections to form a tube. Complete the pinning of the seams. Tack the sections together but curve the tacking in about $\frac{1}{4}''$ from the pinning at the centre of each seam (Figure 58). This avoids any vertical fullness when inserting the lining, which will bow in slightly from the frame Test for fit before machining the seams, the lining should appear slightly tight (see page 32). When the fit is satisfactory machine the seams, remove the tackings and trim the seams to $\frac{1}{8}''$.

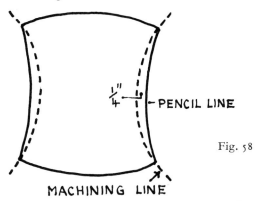

PENCIL LINE

Fig. 58

MACHINING LINE

8. Insert the lining inside the frame and pin the top and bottom of each seam to the top and bottom of a strut.

9. Slash along the top edge of the lining to $\frac{1}{2}''$ from the pencil line but at the fittings slash $\frac{1}{8}''$ below the pencil line. Increase this slash if necessary to remove any wrinkles. Pin every $\frac{1}{2}''$ along the top ring ensuring that A1–D1, A2–D2, etc., fit on the ring.

10. Pin the bottom of the lining to the bottom of the ring, tightening against the top ring.

11. Stitch the material to the rings, the stitching being on the outside of the frame.

12. Trim away the surplus material to $\frac{1}{8}''$.

13. Make and attach neateners.

Cover

The cover is fitted in four separate sections, each being fitted exactly as for the lining and then stitched into position before the next is fitted. It is usual to fit opposite panels but not essential. It is, however, essential that the material is trimmed very closely along the struts. In addition the stitches should only pick up a small piece of material on the struts to avoid having to use a wide trimming to neaten the struts, which will give the shade a clumsy appearance. The surplus material at the rings is rolled back (Figure 24).

Trimming

The struts are trimmed before the rings and this trimming should be as tailored as possible. A narrow velvet ribbon, or narrow strip of the plain fabric, either are very suitable (see Chapter 29).

Suggested Quantities

Bowed Drum, squared base (Plate 13a)
Diameter $11\frac{1}{2}''$, height $9\frac{1}{2}''$.
Cover: 2 panels $12'' \times 12''$, design to be central. $\frac{1}{3}$yd. plain fabric, panels and trimming.
Lining: $\frac{2}{3}$yd. 36'' material.

40

9

Concave Shade with Panelled Cover [Plate 15(c)]

THIS SHADE is, in principle, very similar to the previous shade but emphasises the importance of tightening in the correct direction. If the shade is to be a success the completed shade must have kept the shape of the frame with the centre of each panel as concave as the frame at each ring.

Prepare the frame as for the square bowed drum (page 38).

LINING

This is constructed in the same way as that for the previous shade after very careful fitting.

To Fit

1. Place the lining over the frame with the right side uppermost. Pin at the mid-points of the top and bottom rings, i.e. M and N. Tighten between these two points and this line must be the line of the grain of the material (Figure 59).

N.B. The different positions of the starting points in this shade from the previous shade and the different direction of the tightening.

2. Working outwards from M and N pin the fabric to the top and bottom of the panel, i.e. along the rings, tightening all the time to maintain the curve in the panel.

The tightening on all curved panels is parallel to the straight edges; in this case the struts (Figure 59) and not across the curve as with the previous shade.

3. When the ring sections are fully pinned, roll the sides of the fabric over the struts

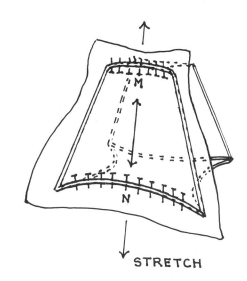

Fig. 59

and pin without any tightening. It is horizontal stretch at this stage which will cause the shape of the panel to be lost.

4. Mark, trim and remove as in the previous shade (page 39, paragraphs 4–6). Continue the assembly of the lining as for this

shade (page 39, paragraphs 7–13). Insert the lining and stitch the top and bottom to the outside of the rings.

An alternative method of lining this shade would be to use an external lining fitted and attached as the cover below.

COVER

1. Fit each panel exactly as the lining panel was fitted (paragraphs 1–4, above), centralising the design if any.

2. Stitch each panel into position as it is fitted to the frame, keeping the stitches on the top or bottom of the ring sections and on the outside of the struts. Take care when stitching the cover to the struts not to accidentally tighten the material horizontally.

3. Trim away the surplus material very carefully from the struts. When all four panels are attached roll back the extra material at the top and bottom and neaten (Figure 24).

TO TRIM

1. The neatening of the struts should be just wide enough to cover the stitches. It is very easy to spoil this style of shade by making or choosing a trimming which is too heavy.

2. Secure a length of the trimming to one end of a strut, the stitches being on the outside of the frame. Tighten it and secure to the opposite end of the strut. With some types of trimming the tautness of the strip will hold it in position without further stitching. Sometimes a little adhesive, applied with a pin, will help anchor it or it may be necessary to stitch it (Figures 27a, b).

3. Neaten the top and bottom rings with a matching trimming.

10

Drum Shades with Tailored Covers

[Plates 2B, 4, 6, 19]

DRUM SHADES, whether round or oval, are very popular designs and with reasonable care are probably two of the easiest to work. Certainly they present few difficulties if the fitting is done carefully and the lining is tested for fit before it is finally inserted.

A true drum has the upper and lower rings the same diameter but with many drum lampshade frames the top ring is often slightly smaller than the bottom one. These tapered frames are easier to store as they will stack easily. True drums and tapered drums are fitted in the same way, but with the latter type the grain of the material will not follow the line of the rings, but will drop at each end (Figure 61). It is important in these shades that the material is fitted symmetrically otherwise the horizontal threads will not meet the seams at the same angle and puckers may appear at the seam during the attaching of the lining or cover to the frame (see Figures 41a, b). Tapered frames are therefore not ideal for striped or checked materials and certainly not for panels of pulled or drawn thread work (Chapter 28, page 111).

FITTING THE LINING OR COVER

This style of frame always has the cover or lining fitted on the straight of the grain (see page 27, paragraph 5).

1. Prepare the frame by painting, binding the rings and two opposite struts.

2. Lie the frame on its side and place the material, wrong side uppermost, over half of it, i.e. from bound strut to bound strut. The grain must run from the centre of the top ring to the centre of the bottom ring (from M to N). Tighten between these two points (Figures 60, 61).

3. Place temporary pins at the top and

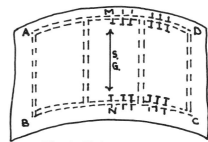

Fig. 60 Fitting a True Drum

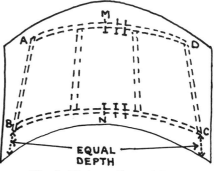

Fig. 61 Fitting a Tapered Drum

bottom of the struts AB and CD. If the drum tapers the grain will not run down these two struts, it is important to see that the material drops equally at B and C (see above and Figure 61).

4. Working outwards from M and N pin towards the two struts AB and CD, tightening between these two rings so that the material is very firm and taut.

5. When half the drum is pinned along the two rings roll the material over the two bound struts and pin about every inch. Do NOT tighten at all horizontally. This is very important when fitting material onto a drum frame. Many drum shades are spoiled as they lose their shape by horizontal tightening. They become round at the top and bottom and hexagonal or octagonal (depending on the number of struts) in the middle (Figure 62).

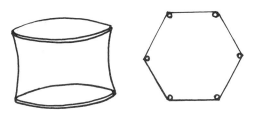

Fig. 62. Front view and cross-section through the middle of the shade showing the effect of tightening the cover horizontally during fitting

6. With a pencil or chalk mark very lightly along the two pinned struts and the top ring, also $\frac{1}{2}''$ at each end of the bottom ring (Figure 63). Trim the surplus material to $1''$ and remove the pins.

TO ASSEMBLE

(A) LINING

Because the lining is fitted on the straight of the grain and on the outside of the frame

it must be made smaller if it is to be used as an internal lining (see Chapter 6, page 31).

7a. Place the marked panel onto the remainder of the fabric, right sides together, and matching the grain exactly.

8a. Pin the materials together, the pins being on the two pencilled lines AB and CD. Now draw an inner line coming in from the original line $\frac{1}{8}''-\frac{1}{4}''$ at the top and bottom of the struts and curving inwards so that it is $\frac{3}{8}''-\frac{1}{2}''$ away at the centre of the lines AB and CD. The thicker the wire the greater the reduction necessary. Tack with small stitches (Figure 63).

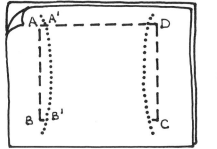

Fig. 63

9a. Tailor tack along the line of the top ring, i.e. AD—snip through these tacks.

10a. Machine along the line A^1B^1 extending the stitching $1''$ at each end of the seam —trim this seam to $\frac{1}{8}''$ and the other tacked seam C^1D^1 to $\frac{1}{2}''$.

11a. Remove the binding from the two struts. Insert the lining to test for size. Pin the seams to the top and bottom of the two struts nearest to the fittings and then pin at the top and bottom of each remaining strut. At the top it is necessary to roll the extra material inside the frame to avoid slashing at the fitting at this stage, i.e. until the fit is correct. The lining should appear to jump from strut to strut and be tight when the hands press it to the frame. Then when it is

44

finally fitted it will roll over the ring with no fullness. If necessary adjust the tacking line of the strut C^1D^1 until a perfect fit is obtained and then machine on the tacking line. Remove the tacking stitches from the two side seams. *N.B.* This may seem a laborious task but it will be amply repaid by the excellence of the final result and with experience the first tacking will be the correct one.

12a. Reinsert the lining, pinning at the top and bottom of the seams—slash at the fittings (Figure 48) and complete the pinning of the top ring. Pin the lower ring tightening against the top ring.

13a. Stitch on the outside of the rings (see page 33, paragraph 6 and Figures 23a, b).

14. Make and attach the neateners (Figures 31, 32).

(B) COVER

7b. As for the lining (7a, page 44).

8b. Fit the two materials together—right sides facing, pin on the pencilled line and tack just outside this line. Machine ON the pencilled lines extending the machining 1″ at each end.

9b. Tailor tack the top ring line.

10b. Slide the cover over the frame, matching the seams of the cover and lining and fitting the tailor tacks to the top ring.

11b. Pin along the top ring and then tighten to the lower ring and pin.

N.B. In a tapered frame it is possible to pull the cover too far down and the rounded shape of the shade will be lost (Figure 62). The tailor tacks in this particular style of shade must not be pulled off the top ring.

12b. Stitch the cover in position—the stitches being on the top or bottom of the rings to cover the stitches of the lining. Roll back the surplus material (Figure 24).

13b. Cut away the surplus fabric and trim as desired.

Suggested Quantities Cover or Lining
Shade: Diameter of Lower Ring up to 11″.
  (i) Height 8″ or less: $\frac{1}{4}$yd. of 36″ material.
  (ii) Height 9″–11″: $\frac{1}{3}$yd. of 36″ material.
  Diameter of Lower Ring 12″–22″.
  (i) Height 8″ or less: $\frac{1}{2}$yd. of 36″ material. (in 2 strips of 9″ × 36″ —one for each half of the shade).
  (ii) Height 9″–11″: $\frac{2}{3}$yd. of 36″ material. (in 2 strips of 12″ × 36″).
  (iii) Height 12″–16″: 1yd. of 36″ material. (in 2 strips of 18″ × 36″).

Candle Shade: Diameter of Ring up to 5″.
  (i) Height $4\frac{1}{2}$″–5″: 2 shades from $\frac{1}{6}$yd. Each shade requires a strip 18″ × 6″.

II

Drum Shades with Pleated Covers [Plates 10A & 10B]

THIS IS a very popular way of treating drum frames. Although when viewing the finished shade it may appear very ambitious, in fact a novice can attempt the shade with confidence. All that is required is accuracy and a little patience. Chiffon and georgette are two of the easiest materials to use; they are easy to handle and are not bulky when pleated. These fabrics should not however be ironed before they are used. Ironing will remove the crinkles from the material making it appear larger (Figure 64).

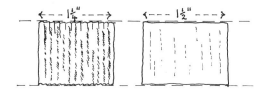

Fig. 64

Before ironing   After ironing

When, however, the shade is subsequently washed, the material will revert to its original texture; it will shrink and the pleats will almost disappear except just at the rings where they are anchored. Whenever possible these materials should be torn and not cut. It is not easy to cut them and achieve a smooth edge. If scissors have to be used have someone hold the material quite taut and slide the scissors through it.

Pleated shades are most successful if lined.

This lining can be used to give a variation of the final effect (Plate 10B(c)). Here the cover is white chiffon, and spaced pleating was used over a deep pink lining. The chiffon muted the colour of the lining but it showed through the single layer of chiffon between the pleats to give an attractive candy-stripe effect. An external lining can be used if the cover is of very sheer material such as some of the nylon chiffons. These would allow the struts to show through the pleating and so mar the finished appearance of the shade. This lining would be fitted and assembled as the cover in Chapter 10. Obviously it is fitted before the pleating can be begun—it is important with this type of lining under a pleated cover that the surplus material at the rings is not trimmed away before the pleating is done (see paragraph 9a, page 48). Alternatively an internal lining may be used—this is usual in shades with touching pleats. A tailored internal lining would be fitted as the lining in Chapter 10. On some occasions both types of lining are used, e.g. if the cover is very sheer and at the same time it is wished to hide the struts. Another occasion would be if a cover of dark material with touching pleats was being used over a pale lining. Very thin hair-line gaps tend to develop between the touching pleats as they are tightened during stitching. If the lining is of a similar colour to the cover these gaps do not show, but over a pale lining they spoil the appearance of the shade when the bulb is lit. This can be avoided by using a dark interlining to match the pleats.

With this type of shade sometimes difficulty is experienced in obtaining suitable trimmings and the selvedges of the material can then be used with success. Plate 13C. It is wise when this may be the case to tear off $\frac{1}{2}''$ – $\frac{3}{4}''$ wide before the material is torn into strips for pleating.

TRUE DRUM WITH SPACED PLEATS

Prepare the frame as in Chapter 2. This is a case where in an unlined shade the rings, having been bound with tape, can be over-bound with strips of the chiffon. Page 10.

Lining

This is prepared before the pleating is begun. If it is to be an external lining it is attached immediately but not trimmed at the rings. If it is to be an internal lining it is inserted after the pleating has been completed. If it was inserted before, the strain

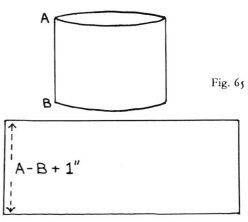

Fig. 65

$2\frac{1}{8} \times$ CIRCUMFERENCE

on the frame during the tightening of the pleats may cause it to slacken.

Spaced Pleating

Allow $2\frac{1}{8} \times$ circumference of the frame by height plus $1''$ (Figure 65).

When using chiffon or any material with a texture running parallel to the selvedge the strips should be torn from selvedge to selvedge. The texture helps to keep the pleats on the grain of the material and moreover the texture would be lost if the tightening was at right angles to it. The depth of the

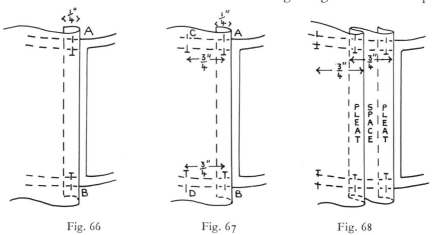

Fig. 66   Fig. 67   Fig. 68

pleats may vary according to personal taste and the size of the shade.

To commence pleating; pleats for this shade to be $\frac{1}{4}''$ wide for ease of description.

1. Tear a strip of material the depth of the shade plus $1''$ in width.

2. Turn under the end $\frac{1}{4}''$ of the material and place over a strut (Figure 66). Pin to the top and bottom ring.

3. Pin $\frac{3}{4}''$ from the front edge of this first pleat on both rings, CA = DB = $\frac{3}{4}''$ (Figure 67).

the top ring and then tightening to the bottom ring as stitching proceeds. As the material is tightened the pleats will go quite flat.

7. Tear a second strip of material and fold under $\frac{1}{4}''$ (see paragraph 2 above) and place this over the last $\frac{1}{4}''$ of the previous strip (Figure 69). Continue the pleating until the cover is complete. Tear off any surplus material from the last strip so that $\frac{1}{4}''$ remains to be slipped under the first pleat (see paragraphs 2 and 6 above).

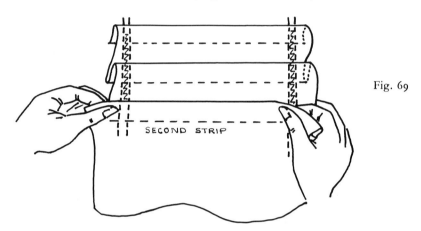

Fig. 69

SECOND STRIP

4. Fold back the material $\frac{1}{4}''$ from these pins C and D and pin—this should leave a space of $\frac{1}{4}''$ between the pleats (Figure 68).

5. Repeat this procedure until the first strip of chiffon has been used, finishing at Stage 2 shown in Figure 67—paragraph 3 above. Trim off any surplus chiffon beyond points C and D, i.e. $\frac{3}{4}''$ from the front edge of the last pleat.

6. Stitch this section into position but leave the first two pleats unstitched (see paragraph 7 below). It is an advantage to stitch each section as soon as it is pinned in order to keep the number of pins in the shade at any one time to a minimum. Stitch on the outside of the rings, attaching the material first to

8. Complete the stitching and trim away the surplus material at the rings, trimming right back to the stitches.

For Shades with External Lining Only

9a. Roll the surplus material of the lining up over the stitches securing the pleating (see above).

10a. Stitch this material in position (Figure 24) and trim away any excess fabric.

For Shades with Internal Lining

9b. If an external or interlining has been used trim away any surplus fabric from pleating and external lining.

10b. Insert the lining as Chapter 10.

TRUE DRUM WITH TOUCHING PLEATS

Allow $3\frac{1}{4}$ × circumference of the frame by height plus 1″.

With touching pleats $\frac{1}{4}$″ is rather small for the depth of the pleats—$\frac{3}{8}$″ is more successful, but again this is not mandatory.

The material is prepared as for the shade with spaced pleats.

To Work

1. Fold under $\frac{3}{8}$″ and place the fold over a strut.

2. Pin $\frac{3}{4}$″ from the front edge of the first pleat.

3. Fold the material back until it just overlaps the previous pleat and pin—this slight overlap is to prevent gaps appearing between the pleats after tightening when the cover is stitched into position (see page 46 and Figure 70: pins omitted from this figure to show the overlap clearly).

4. Continue the pleating and joining as for the spaced pleated shade but without the spaces.

NB

1. As an aid to even pleating the spacing can be marked on the frame before pleating is begun. A template (Figure 71) is a great help if this method of obtaining even pleats is used.

2. If a worker has a 'good eye' she may be able to work successfully without any measuring.

3. Pleating is most successful if it can be completed in as few sessions as possible. A rhythm is developed during working and this helps to achieve even pleating.

4. It will be noticed that when giving the quantities of material for spaced pleats $2\frac{1}{8}$ × circumference is allowed and $3\frac{1}{4}$ × circumference for the touching pleats. This is more than the arithmetic amounts which would be twice and three times the circumference respectively. It is a fact that due to the nature of the fabric the extra material is used and allowance must be made for this.

5. Some workers prefer to pin the bottom of the pleat and then the top—working with the struts at right angles to the body (Figures 66–68). Others prefer to turn the frame side-

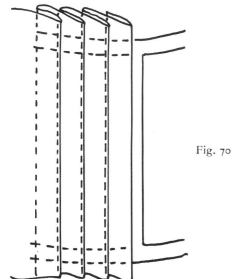

Fig. 70

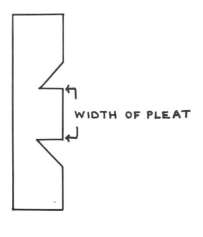

WIDTH OF PLEAT

Fig. 71

ways, i.e. with the struts parallel to the body and complete the pleat in one operation (Figure 69).

The correct method is the one which is found to be the easiest to the individual—the one with which she can obtain the best results.

6. The accuracy of the pleating is checked as each strut is reached. The pleat starting at the bottom of a strut should lie over the entire length of the strut.

TAPERED SHADES

These are a very common style of frame (see page 43). They require a little more care as the pleats are not parallel but a little closer together on the top ring than on the bottom, hence the method of pleating must be slightly adjusted. It is not practical to measure or mark along the top ring so this is done along the bottom ring only; if in fact the marking method is used (see *N.B.* Page 49, paragraph 1).

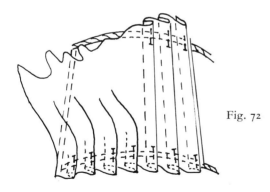

Fig. 72

To Work

1. Work as for the true drum but pin the pleats along the bottom ring only whether spaced or touching pleats. Work one panel at a time (i.e. between one pair of struts only).

2. Work with the bottom ring to the body. Pleat under $\frac{1}{4}''$ or $\frac{3}{8}''$, depending on the size of pleat, and pin to the top ring for the first pleat, the pleat lying over a strut.

3. From the second pleat on the bottom ring fold the material along the grain (the texture will help here) and fix the pleat to the top ring so that the pleat is at right angles to the bottom ring (Figure 72). The fact that the pleat must be at 90° to the lower ring is a great help with this tapered frame. Automatically pleats made in this way will be closer together on the top ring than on the lower ring.

N.B. It is important to check the line of the pleat at each strut; it must run up the strut.

These frames are then completed as the true drums.

PLEATED LINING—Plate 1e

These linings are very attractive when the lining of the shade can easily be seen as in a pendant shade and in particular in a wide drum as Plate 10A. Jap silk is a very suitable choice for such a lining as it is not bulky when pleated.

Spaced pleating is more suitable for linings than touching pleats as it is daintier and of course more economical. If used under a cover of spaced pleats great care must be taken that the pleats of the lining and the cover coincide. It is really most effective under a dark cover of touching pleats (Plate 10A. Care is needed when fixing the pleats to the top ring at the junction with the fitting; the slash is usually through three thicknesses which is finished with a neatener (Figures 31, 32). The lining is taken to the outside of the frame for stitching so that the stitches are hidden by the trimming.

VARIATIONS OF PLEATING

Two very simple pleating arrangements have been described, but it is interesting to experiment with others such as the grouped pleats in Figure 73 and the box pleats in Figure 74. The box pleats can have their edges caught together to give a smocked or honeycomb effect. The shade in Plate 10B (d) had tiny pearls holding the edges of the pleats together and a pearl trimming was used to neaten the rings. Another variation is to use larger pleats with a heavier material— wild silk—this shade can be finished with pieces of ribbon fastened between the pleats 2″ from the lower ring. Plate 23. The neatenings of the rings is then kept very simple— e.g. matching velvet ribbon ⅜″ wide (see Chapter 29, page 117).

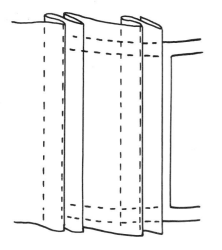

Fig. 73

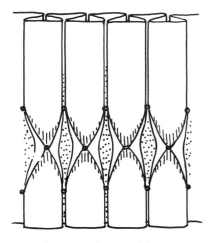

Fig. 74—Plate 10B[e]

Suggested Quantities
Linings

Plain linings. Allow the same quantitites as for a shade of similar size as given for a Tailored Shade in Chapter 10.

Lining of spaced pleats. Double the above amount.

Covers

Diameter of lower ring less than 13″.

    (i) Spaced pleating. Double the quantity given for the Tailored Cover in Chapter 10, but use 44″ chiffon instead of 36″ material (see page 45).

    (ii) Touching pleats. Treble the quantities given in Chapter 10 again using 44″ chiffon.

Diameter 14″–17″

Spaced pleats: Allow 3 strips of 44″ chiffon—each the length of 1 strut + 1″.

Touching pleats: Allow 4 strips.

Diameter 18″–24″

Spaced pleats: Allow 4 strips.

Touching pleats: Allow 5 strips for 18″, 20″ and 22″ shade and 6 strips for a 24″ shade.

12

Fluted Drum Shade [Plate 9a]

THIS IS a very attractive frame and it is seen at its best when fitted with a pleated cover. Small pleats—$\frac{1}{4}''$ or $\frac{3}{8}''$ maximum—are the most suitable because of the curved nature of the frame. These frames are almost always tapered.

The pleating is worked exactly as that on the plain drum frames (Figure 72) but a different type of internal lining is usually fitted; one which is very simple to construct and easy to fit and attach.

To Work

1. Prepare the frame by painting with a paint matching the colour of the lining and by binding the rings with tape. It is not necessary to bind any struts even temporarily.

2. Pleat the cover (touching pleats give the most attractive result with this type of frame); for method see pages 49, 50. Trim.

3. The lining.

(a) Measure the outside of the frame accurately, going carefully into the flutes of the frame. This measurement will be more than $3\frac{1}{7}$ times the diameter of the ring (Figure 75). e.g. The shade in Plate 9. Maximum diameter of the ring 10". Circumference of the ring $33\frac{1}{4}''$.

(b) Tear a strip of material equal to the length of one strut plus $1\frac{1}{2}''$ in depth.

The length of the strip should be that of the circumference of the frame plus $\frac{1}{2}''$ for seam allowance. If this measurement is less than the width of the material (usually 36") the lining can be cut in one piece. If the measurement exceeds 36" the lining strip should be made up from two pieces of material (Figure 76). Join the material to form a cylinder—a single seam is adequate.

(c) Divide the cylinder into a number

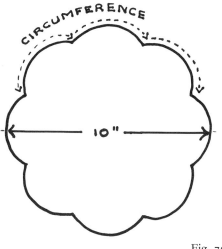

Fig. 75

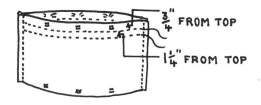

Fig. 76

of sections to correspond with the number of struts—mark these divisions with tailor-tacking threads on both edges of the lining (Figure 76).

(d) Run two rows of gathering threads along one edge—$\frac{3}{4}''$ and $1\frac{1}{4}''$ from the edge of the fabric (Figure 76).

(e) With wrong side outermost, slide the lining over the outside of the shade—the edge without the gathering threads to the bottom ring. Pin the tailor-tack marks on the ungathered edge to the bottom of the struts. Put extra pins, about $\frac{1}{2}''$ apart, round the bottom ring (Figure 77).

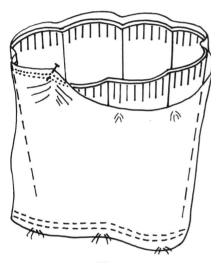

Fig. 77

(f) Stitch on the outside of the ring and trim any excess material back to the ring.

(g) Turn the lining to the inside of the shade—it will roll over the lower ring of the frame and so neaten the lower edge of the pleating. When stitching the pleats into position with this style of shade the stitches should be on the bottom of the ring so that they will be hidden by the lining.

(h) Pin the tailor-tack marks on the top edge of the lining to the top of the struts, at the same time tightening the lining against the lower ring.

(i) Draw up the gathering threads carefully, spacing the gathers evenly.

(j) Pin every $\frac{1}{2}''$ along the top ring, still tightening against the lower ring and slashing as necessary at the fittings (Figure 48), being careful not to snip the gathering threads. Remove any gathering thread which is below the top ring after pinning.

(k) Stitch the lining very firmly to the outside of the top ring. Trim away any surplus material and attach neateners at the fittings.

The shade is now ready for trimming. With this method of inserting the lining it is not essential to add a trimming to the lower edge—this is optional.

Suggested Quantities

Diameter of Lower Ring up to 10".
  Height up to 8": Lining, $\frac{1}{4}$yd. of 36" material.
  Cover, spaced pleats: $\frac{1}{2}$yd. of 44" chiffon (2 strips of 9" × 44").
    touching pleats: $\frac{3}{4}$yd. of 44" chiffon (3 strips of 9" × 44").

Diameter of Lower Ring 11" or 12".
  Height up to 8": Lining, $\frac{1}{2}$yd. of 36" material.
  Cover, spaced pleats, $\frac{1}{2}$yd. of 44" chiffon.
    touching pleats, $\frac{3}{4}$yd. of 44" chiffon.

Diameter of Lower Ring 20".
  Height of frame 12"–16": Lining, 1yd. (2 strips of 18" × 36").
  Cover, spaced pleats, 4 strips 13"–17" in depth × 44".
    touching pleats, 5 strips the required depth.

I3

Simple Pleated or Gathered Empire Shade

[Plate 10A(a)]

THE FRAME for this shade may be the simple straight-sided empire style or it may have a collar or stand at the top edge (Figures 5c, 79 and 80). Occasionally one meets these shades with only four struts and this is one of the few designs for which they can be used successfully (page 26). The final shape does not rely on the position or number of the struts.

It is a very simple shade to make and it can be made with or without a lining. If it is decided to use a lining this can be made very easily as a copy of the cover and this type of lining should be used if the frame has a collar. In a simple empire frame a balloon lining (Chapter 6) can be substituted for the pleated lining described later in this chapter.

As there is no fullness at the lower edge there is relatively little at the top ring or rings and so a more substantial material can be used if desired. Jap silk, crêpe-backed satin, tussore, shantung and novelty cottons such as Robia can be used for the cover.

UNLINED SHADE

Prepare the frame. Paint the whole frame, bind all the rings (2 or 3) but no struts. The struts tend to disappear into the pleats. The binding must match the cover.

Cover

Tear a strip of material; the length being

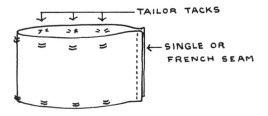

Fig. 78

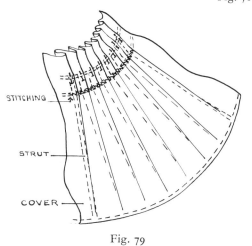

Fig. 79

equal to the circumference of the lower ring plus $\frac{1}{2}''$ for seam allowance and the width being the length of a strut (or strut plus collar—Figure 79) plus 2″ for ease of working at the top ring.

If the circumference of the frame is less than 36″, i.e. the diameter of the lower ring is 11″ or less, then the fabric can be cut in one piece. If the frame is 12″ or more in dia-

54

meter the cover should be made of two equal pieces and the seams placed over two struts (as in Figure 76).

To Assemble

1. Join the two short ends of the material with a narrow French seam, not more than $\frac{1}{8}''$ wide ($\frac{1}{2}''$ allowed for seam).

2. Mark with tailor tacks the position of the struts on both edges of the material (Figure 78).

3. Place the cover INSIDE the frame with the right side of the material to the frame. The edge of the material should be level with the edge of the ring. Pin one set of tailor tacks to the bottom of each strut—the cover will have just a slight amount of fullness as it has been fitted to the outside of the frame and it has to roll over the ring back to the outside of the shade. Complete the pinning of the lower ring.

4. Stitch (Figures 23a, b) to the inside of the ring. Trim.

5. Roll the cover over the bottom ring— the material will now be right side outside.

6. Pin the tailor tacks at the top edge of the material to the top of the struts—there will be some fullness between each pair of pins. If the frame has a collar, pin to the lower of the two rings.

7. Dispose the fullness in the form of pleats evenly spaced and arrange one pleat over each strut (Figure 79).

8. Stitch to the ring. If there is a collar continue the pleats to the top ring, the pleats being parallel. Stitch to the top ring (Figure 79).

9. The shade is now ready for trimming. It is not essential to trim the lower ring as it will automatically be neatened when the cover is rolled over it in paragraph 5. Where there is a collar both rings will require trimming.

N.B. A circular needle is helpful when stitching to the lower ring of a collar.

LINED SHADES

Prepare the frame as for the unlined shade.

Lining and Cover

These are identical and are prepared in the same way as the cover for the unlined shade except that a French seam is not necessary, a single seam in each will be adequate.

To Assemble

1. Slide the cover, right side outermost, over the frame.

2. Pin one tailor tack to the bottom of each strut and then complete the pinning of the cover to the bottom ring. The lower edge of the material should be $\frac{1}{8}''$ below the ring.

3. Stitch to the bottom of the ring.

4. Fit the top of the cover to the top ring or collar as in the unlined shade (paragraphs 6–8) and complete the stitching (Figure 79).

5. If there is a collar it is easier to trim the lower ring of this collar at this stage, before the lining is attached.

6. Slide the lining, WRONG side outermost, over the shade (Figure 77).

7. Pin this to the frame in the same way as the cover.

8. Stitch to the outside of the bottom ring; when the lining is taken to the inside of the shade it will hide the stitches securing the cover to the ring.

9. Roll the lining over the bottom ring and bring up inside the frame to the top ring. Pin one set of tailor tacks to the top of each strut, tightening the material against the bottom ring, again there will be fullness which will be formed into pleats (Figure 80).

Even if there is a collar the lining will be

taken directly to the top ring. There is no need to fit or stitch to the lower ring of the collar as the material will bend over it in a convex curve (Figure 80).

10. Stitch the lining to the top edge of the top ring.

Trim the top ring making sure the trim-

ming rolls over the top ring so hiding any stitches.

N.B. Gathers can replace the pleats on the top ring or collar. In this case two rows of gathering threads should be worked on both lining and cover as on the lining for the Fluted Drum (Figure 76). If there is a collar there should be four rows of gathering threads. This gathered finish may be used on lined and unlined shades.

Suggested Quantities. Lining or Cover.
  Diameter of Lower Ring up to 11".
    (i) Length of strut and collar (if any) not more than 8": ¼yd. of 36" material.
    (ii) Length of strut and collar 9"–11": ⅓yd. of 36" material.

Diameter of Lower Ring 20"–22" (Standard Lamp Shade).
  Length of Strut and collar up to 17": 1yd. of 36" material (2 strips 18" × 36").

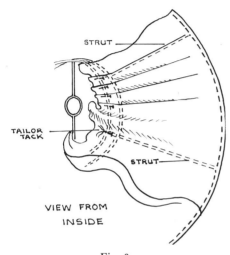

Fig. 80

14

Panelled Shade with Pleated Ends [Plates 7 & 13c]

THIS SHADE allows for the combination of two materials; these may differ in texture or design. If patterned material was used on all the panels the impact of the design would be lost as in the shade in Chapter 8. The shades in Plates 13a and c used the same glazed chintz for the central panels but chiffon was used for the pleating on the end panels. In 13b the chiffon picked up one of the colours in the design on the chintz.

Preparation

Paint the whole frame. Bind the four struts adjacent to the central panels and the two rings. Temporarily bind the end struts to allow for the lining to be fitted.

Lining

This is fitted on the straight of the fabric and may be attached internally or externally. *N.B.* If the lining is to be attached externally ALL the struts should be bound to match the lining. Where an internal lining is fitted it is attached before the external lining and cover even though the latter is partially pleated (see paragraph 9 below).

1. Commence by placing the material, wrong side outside, over half the frame. Leave at least 1″ of material beyond each ring to allow for the drop at each end (Figure 81).

2. On both rings place a pin at the midpoints (M and N) of one central panel. Pin

along both rings tightening vertically, i.e. parallel to the straight struts.

3. On reaching the strut AB continue pinning along the rings to P and Q.

4. When pinning the material to the strut PQ tighten against the lower ring, i.e. vertically (Figure 81). Work from M and N to the strut opposite to PQ.

5. Mark very faintly with a pencil along the top ring and both outside struts. Remove the pins. Remove the temporary binding (see *Preparation* above) from the two end struts—this does not apply if an external lining only is used.

6. Place the marked panel over the spare

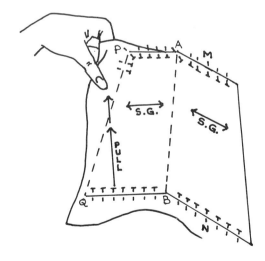

Fig. 81

material, matching the grain very carefully and prepare the lining as for the lining of the Tailored Drum (Chapter 10, pages 44–45). Tack both seams but do not machine either.

7. Test for fit of the lining; if it is to be inserted inside the frame, again it should be tight. If adjustment is necessary it must be made on BOTH seams and not one as in the case of the drum shade. This is so that the lining will remain symmetrical about the line M–N. This seam should be double machined—the two rows being about $\frac{1}{8}''$ apart (see paragraph 9 below). Trim up to the outer line of machining.

8. Tailor tack the line of the top ring and snip through these tacks.

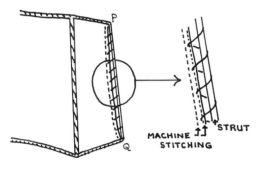

Fig. 82

9. Insert the lining. Pin the line of the tailor tacks to the top ring, slashing at the fittings. Turn the shade to sit on its top ring and tighten the lining to the bottom ring. Occasionally this lining can present problems in removing all vertical wrinkles. These may appear after the lining seems quite taut. In these cases the fault can be corrected by catching the side seams to the end struts. This is a technique very rarely used, but with this particular frame it will give a perfect result which may otherwise be difficult to obtain. A fine thread is used and the stitches

pass between the two rows of machining (paragraph 7 above) and round the end strut which is unbound. The lining then becomes taut—care must be taken not to overtighten (Figure 82).

10. Stitch the lining to the outsides of both rings.

11. Trim away any surplus material and attach neateners (Figure 32).

COVER

1. Fit the two central panels first. Commence the pinning as for the lining (paragraph 2, page 57) but fit only as far as the inner struts AB and CD, tightening vertically.

2. Pin down these two struts but with NO horizontal tightening—this would remove the curve from the fabric panel (see page 41).

3. Stitch along the top of the top ring and then to the bottom of the lower ring, tightening as the stitching proceeds.

Stitch the fabric to the struts, keeping the stitches to the outside of the frame and with no tightening.

4. The pleated ends. This pleating is worked in two sections; both sections being pleated towards the strut PQ—see trimming, page 59. For touching pleats, tear a strip of chiffon 3 × the length of the lower ring section QB plus 2″ and in height equal to the strut PQ plus 1″.

5. Make a double turning of $\frac{3}{8}''$ wide and place over the end of the central panel, i.e. over AB, completely covering the stitches on the strut and any raw edges (Figure 83b). Pin touching pleats $\frac{3}{8}''$ wide along the ring QB and finish with a single layer of the material over the strut PQ (Figure 83a). Trim off any excess length. Complete the pleating to the top ring as for the tapered drum (Chapter 11, paragraphs 1–3 and

58

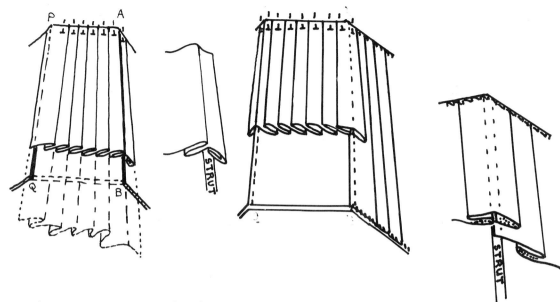

Fig. 83a Fig. 83b
Showing cross-section through the material on
the right-hand panel

Fig. 84a Fig. 84b
Showing enlargement of the join of the
left-hand panel

Figure 72). Stitch the chiffon to both rings, keeping it very tight. Trim off any spare material at the rings.

6. Tear off a second strip of chiffon but make it 1″ longer than the first.

7. Begin this pleating from the edge of the opposite central panel and again work to the strut PQ but with the pleats facing away from this strut. Work as for the first half (paragraph 5; Figure 84a).

8. The last of these pleats should finish at the strut PQ. Measure $\frac{3}{4}$″ beyond this pleat and tear off any chiffon in excess of this amount (Figures 84a, b).

9. Fold under the last $\frac{3}{8}$″ of the material and this should lie over the last $\frac{3}{8}$″ of the first section of the pleating—paragraph 5. This will make a box pleat over the end strut PQ (Figure 84b). Stitch the pleats to both rings keeping the material very taut. Work the opposite two panels in the same way.

TRIMMING

The shade is now ready for trimming. Because of the arrangement of the pleats with the outside pleats overlapping the edges of the patterned panels there is no need of any trimming other than that on the two rings. This trimming should be quite simple as the patterned panels and the pleating are the interesting features of this shade.

Suggested Quantities
Shade, base at widest part 14″, height 9″.
  Lining: $\frac{1}{3}$yd. 36″ material. (Very economical fitting necessary.)
  Cover: 2 panels 11″ × 12″ (design to be central.) $\frac{2}{3}$yd. 44″ chiffon (2 pieces 12″ × 44″).

59

15

Swathed Pleated Shades [Plates 10A & 10B]

THESE SHADES probably call for more care than other styles of pleated shades but the result is ample repayment for the patience expended. There is a choice of methods of working the swathing; one requires little preparation but great care in working, the second needs some preliminary tacking of the material before pleating is begun but is a very successful method for the novice.

CHOICE OF FRAME

For swathed shades a bowed frame should be used (see Chapter 1, paragraph f). This allows the pleats to sweep across the frame in an unbroken line. The bowed empire frame may be round or oval.

LININGS

Swathed shades need lining to neaten the joins of the strips of chiffon or georgette and to give body to the cover. With the sheer fabrics necessary for this technique of swathing an external lining is often necessary to hide the struts and is frequently used in conjunction with an internal lining. If touching pleats are used along the lower ring, this internal lining is not usually necessary.

For shades where there is no risk of the lining being too close to the bulb, an internal lining fitted on the cross is usually easier to insert. The tightening of the swathing around the shade often slightly alters the shape of the frame and if the lining has been cut on the cross it is more easily adjusted. If, however, a lining cut on the straight of the fabric is used it is most important to test it for fit (see page 31) AFTER the swathing has been completed.

COVER

This may be made with either spaced or touching pleats along the bottom ring. However as the top ring in a bowed empire frame is considerably smaller than the bottom ring the pleats will overlap quite considerably at the top ring, so producing bulk. For this reason it is often more successful to have spaced pleating along the lower ring. In addition the effect when the bulb is lit is very attractive as the spaces gradually decrease and the pleats eventually meet.

Estimating the quantity of material:

(a) measure the circumference of the ring—this will be $3\frac{1}{7} \times$ the diameter of the shade. For spaced pleating double this measurement to give the total length of the strips of the material used. For touching pleats then the circumference is trebled.

(b) height. Measure the distance from the bottom of one strut to the top of the opposite strut; i.e. the swathing will sweep halfway round the frame. This keeps the material to the shape of the frame. To this measurement add 2″ to give working material at each end of the strip (Figures 87b and 90).

Tear the selvedges off the chiffon: these may be useful as trimmings later. Always tear the material from selvedge to selvedge if it has a crinkled texture (see page 46).

METHODS

Paint the frame and bind both rings. If no internal lining is to be used or spaced pleating is to be used all the struts should be bound to match the external lining (Chapter 2, paragraphs b and c). If two linings or touching pleats are planned then two opposite struts should be bound temporarily to allow the linings to be fitted.

Fit and assemble the lining but do not insert an internal lining at this stage—it would go slack during the tightening of the swathing. An external lining is fitted as the cover in Chapter 6, pages 32 and 33.

To Work: Method I

1. The pleats may either be marked out on the ring and material before working is commenced (Figure 85) or they may be gauged by 'eye' as the work proceeds (see page 49).

2. Pin the pleats to the lower ring for one panel (i.e. between one pair of struts) only, making the pleats $\frac{1}{4}″$, $\frac{3}{8}″$ or $\frac{1}{2}″$ depending on the size of the shade and personal choice. Suppose there are X pleats.

Measure the distance between two struts on the top ring—Y″. Divide this measurement Y by X. Y″/X will be the distance between the front edges of the pleats on the top ring. This should be an aid to anyone who finds it difficult in paragraph 4 below

to arrange all the pleats in the space available. For those with a 'good eye' this calculation will not be necessary.

3. To swathe the first pleat, turn the shade sideways, fold under the raw edge (already folded and pinned at the bottom ring) and swathe the pleat round to the top of the opposite strut. Pin with the pin pointing outwards. The grain of the material should run along the edge of the pleat and the folded edge of the pleat and all subsequent pleats must face downwards (Figure 85). This avoids the pleats trapping dirt, any such dirt will not be removed on washing. The

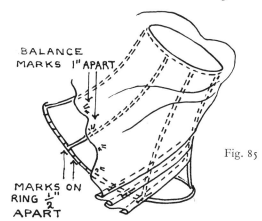

BALANCE MARKS 1″ APART

MARKS ON RING $\frac{1}{2}″$ APART

Fig. 85

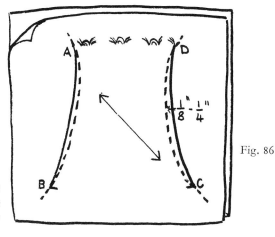

Fig. 86

swathing may be worked in either direction, i.e. to the right or to the left.

4. Continue pleating the material, always on the grain of the material, until all the pleats on the bottom ring of one panel have been completed—pinning each to the top ring as it is made. It is most important that all the pleats from one panel on the bottom ring fit into one panel on the top ring. The pleats on the top ring will be much closer together than on the bottom ring (Figures 85 and 90).

5. Stitch the pleats to the top ring—leave the first 3 or 4 pleats made, unstitched to allow for the joining of the material at the end of the pleating (Chapter 11, paragraphs 6 and 7, page 48). The stitches should be on the top of the ring and close together to anchor the beginning and end of each pleat very securely.

6. Adjust the pleats at the bottom ring—they may have twisted slightly during the swathing. Tighten away from the ring and the pleats will become quite flat. Stitch to the bottom of the lower ring, holding the material as shown in Figure 23a but the left hand will now be holding the pleats. Again leave the first pleat unstitched.

7. Continue the pleating, swathing and the stitching, working a panel at a time and checking that the number of pleats is the same on the top and bottom rings.

8. When it is necessary to join on a new strip of material, do this as for the drum shade (Chapter 11, page 48).

9. Complete the final join as for the above shade.

10. Trim off any surplus fabric from the rings.

11. Test the internal lining for fit (see page 60). Adjust the seams if there is fullness apparent in the middle of the shade. Curve the seams in slightly (Figure 86). No adjustments should be necessary at either the top or the bottom of the seams. When the fit is satisfactory insert the lining—see Chapter 6, pages 32 and 33—and stitch to the outside of the rings thus covering the raw edges of the pleating.

The shade is now ready for trimming.

To Work: Method II

This method may be used by a worker who has very little experience of the craft or no 'eye' for judging the even spacing of pleats. It involves some preparation before beginning the pleating but once this is done the swathing is very simple.

Calculate the height and length of the material as in the previous method.

N.B. The example given below is for a medium-sized frame—8"–12" diameter—and made with eight pleats to each panel. For smaller frames have 4 or 6 pleats and for a standard shade have 12 pleats to a panel.

Tear two strips of material, each to measure the circumference of the frame by the required height, each will cover half the shade.

1. Divide each piece of material into three by use of coloured thread, e.g. red (Figure 87a). There should be no knot at the beginning or back-stitch at the end of the tacking; the thread will then slip out easily when no longer required.

2. Divide each of the 6 sections (3 in each piece of fabric) into eight with contrasting cotton (blue)—there will be seven lines (Figure 87a).

3. On the lower ring divide each section into 8 (Figure 87b), marking with pencil on the outside of the ring. It is not practical to mark the top ring; the pleats there are so close together that the marks would be hidden by the previous pleat. Each pleat will be

an eighth of the length of the panel on the top ring from the pleat in front.

4. Fix one piece of chiffon to the lower ring thus: pin the 2 red tacks and the two ends to 4 struts—and the intervening blue tacks to the pencil marks. There will be some fullness between the pins (Figure 88).

5. Turn the frame sideways with the bottom ring to the right and smooth the fullness forwards, i.e. towards you to form a pleat. Pin it down (Figure 89).

6. Begin with the first formed pleat, continue the pleat up the fabric on the grain of the fabric to the top edge. Sweep the material round to the top of the opposite strut. Tighten in the direction of the pleat and pin (Figure 90). Repeat with the second pleat,

the blue tacking will be $\frac{1}{4}''$–$\frac{1}{2}''$ under the fold depending on the size of the pleat on the ring (Figure 89). The pleats face downwards to prevent dust collecting. Continue pleating until a red thread is reached, this pleat will start from a strut and must go to the top of the opposite strut, thus the accuracy of the pleating is checked every panel. Complete the pinning of the three panels and stitch as for Method I, paragraphs 5 and 6, but remove the tackings before the stitching is begun.

7. Attach the second piece of material in the same way. The first pleat will automatically cover the raw edge of the first half of the cover, and the end of this second piece fits under the first pleat.

8. Trim off the surplus material at the rings and insert the lining as Method I, paragraph 11.

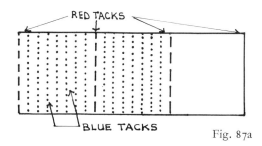

Fig. 87a

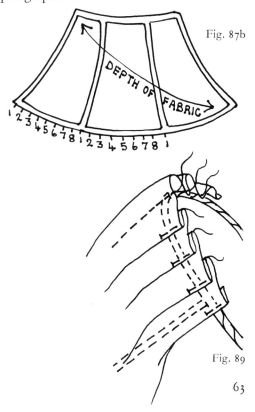

Fig. 87b

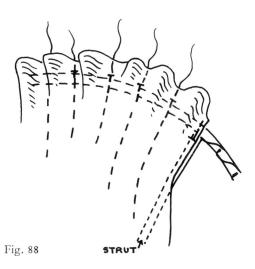

Fig. 88   STRUT

Fig. 89

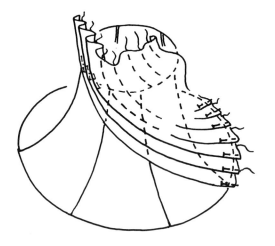

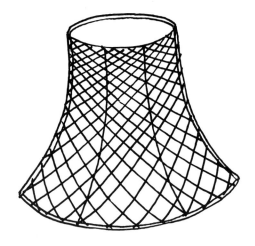

Fig. 90

Fig. 91

CROSS-SWATHED SHADE–Plate 10B(b)

This shade looks particularly lovely when over a light as it gives a honeycomb effect. It is seen at its best when the lining is a deeper tone than the cover.

The cover may be made by either method described earlier in this chapter but spaced pleating should be used along the bottom ring. This avoids a heavy effect and makes the pattern formed by the pleats more interesting. A sheer fabric is essential—nylon chiffon or organza give very good results but need skill in handling. This shade has in fact two layers of swathing, each worked as for a single swathe (see above).

The swathing is worked in both directions, i.e. both to the right and the left. If method II is used to do the pleating the same marks on the bottom ring are used for both layers (paragraph 3) but in paragraph 5 the frame is turned so the bottom ring is to the left, for the second layer, thus ensuring the pleating goes in the opposite direction (Figure 91).

It is not necessary to use an external lining when a cross-swathed cover is made.

Suggested Quantities
10″ shade. Height 7″ (approx.).
  Lining: $\frac{1}{3}$yd. 36″ material (1 lining only —double these quantities if internal and external linings are used).
  Cover: $\frac{3}{4}$yd. 44″ chiffon.

12″–14″ shade. Height 8″–10″.
  Lining: $\frac{1}{2}$yd. 36″ material.
  Cover: 1yd. 44″ chiffon.

Standard shade. 20″ diameter.
  Lining: 1yd. 36″ material.
  Cover: $2\frac{1}{2}$–3yds. depending on the height of a strip. See Figure 87b. One strip covers two panels (6 struts to the shade).

For cross-swathing, double the amounts given for the cover in each case.

16

Shade with Central Ruching [Plate 11(c)]

THIS LOOKS a very ambitious shade and certainly does require care and a certain amount of patience. The main essential for success is a very fine fabric which is not extremely prone to fray. Silk chiffon is the ideal material; nylon chiffon would be too liable to fray. It is most important that the gathering in the centre of the panel is not bulky or the shade loses that daintiness which should be the dominant feature.

CHOICE OF FRAME

The choice of frames is limited by the nature of the tightening of the pleats. Any shade with flat or almost flat panels can be used; the central panels of an oval drum, the central panels of the shade used in Chapter 14, a square shade with cut away corners are all suitable and an oval bowed empire frame can be used with success.

LININGS

This style of shade must have an external lining and preferably an internal lining as well. The external lining has three main functions

(a) to form a base to which the centre of the panel, i.e. the centre of the ruching can be fixed while the whole panel is pinned into position—see paragraph f, page 66.

(b) to give body to the ruched panel; it is of necessity of very sheer material and there will be spaces between the pleats where these are attached to the frame (Figure 95). These spaces are very transparent and the final effect is improved by the presence of an external lining.

(c) in certain shades, where the ruched panel is over a curve as on an oval bowed empire or an oval bowed drum, it helps to preserve the shape of the frame. The pleats otherwise would jump from strut to strut and the curved outline lost. A taut interlining, fitted according to the instructions for curved frames (see Chapters 6 and 10) prevents this from happening.

To Prepare the Frame

Paint the whole frame. Bind both rings and those struts which will have material stitched to them or to which the lining will be fitted.

TO WORK

1. Fit and prepare the internal lining but do not attach.

2. Fit, prepare and attach the external lining. For an empire or drum shade this is fitted as a tailored cover (Chapters 6 and 10). On a panelled frame it is attached panel by panel, each stitched in position and trimmed. The trimmed edges are not, of course, neatened by overcasting. It is important to keep bulk, both on the struts and on the rings, to a minimum.

3. The Cover. This may be prepared in one of two ways.

Method I

The advantage of this method is that the bulk at the centre of the ruching is reduced to a minimum, but an ample amount of fullness remains at the outer edges of the panel.

(a) The oval in the centre of the panel is 2″ longer than the base BC, of the frame and the height is 1″–2″ more than the strut AB. This oval, when removed, can be used for a part of the lining (Figure 93). The minimum depth of the material around the oval is 1″ more than the distance OB; i.e. the distance from the centre of the panel to the furthermost part of the frame to which it is being attached (Figure 92). Faintly outline the oval with pencil (Figure 93).

(b) Work two rows of gathering threads around the oval, one on the pencil line and one $\frac{1}{8}$″ outside it.

(c) Mark the midpoints of the four edges of the material and divide it into quarters with tacking threads but do not take these across the oval (Figure 93).

(d) Mark the half and quarter marks on the frame P, R, S, T. Note that P and S are below the midpoints of the struts AB and CD; that is because AD is less than BC (Figure 92).

(e) Cut out the central oval and draw up the gathering threads very tightly, but carefully, in order not to break the threads or fray the fabric.

(f) Pin and tack the centre of the ruching to the midpoint O of the external lining: this is very important as it ensures that the focal point remains in the centre of the shade during the tightening of the pleats or gathers.

(g) Pin one tacking thread to each quarter mark on the frame, tightening the material away from the centre. There will be fullness all round the panel at this stage (Figure 94).

(h) This fullness is now disposed evenly around the panel as gathers or small pleats.

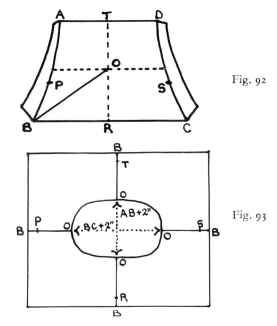

Fig. 92

Fig. 93

If gathers are used a gathering thread can be run around between the points P, R, S, T. If small pleats are formed there should be one placed to each corner (Figure 95). During tightening care must be taken not to pull the centre of the ruching away from the centre of the shade (paragraph f).

(i) When the pinning is complete stitch the panel firmly to the frame and trim away any surplus material.

(j) Fit a second panel in the same way. If a bowed empire frame is being used this will complete the cover. If an angular shade is used then the other panels have still to be completed; these will be fitted as for the sectional shades (Chapters 8, 9, 14).

Method II

(a) Measure around the panel: A-B-C-D-A, and use $1\frac{1}{2}$–2 times this measurement for the length of the strip (Figures 92 and 96). The amount selected depends on the texture of the material being used.

66

The height of the strip is the distance OB plus $1\frac{1}{2}''$ (Figure 92).

(b) Mark out and cut an oblong to these measurements (Figure 96). The strip may have to be joined if it is longer than the width of the fabric: use a single seam.

(c) Mark the quarters on the frame (paragraph d—method I) (Figure 92), also on one long edge of the strip of material (Figure 96).

(d) Run 2 rows of fine gathering stitches, $\frac{1}{8}''$ apart along the other long edge.

(e) Join the two short edges with a single seam.

(f) Draw up the gathering threads very carefully but very tightly. Continue from paragraph (g) in Method I.

The pleats will be a little easier to handle in this method as they will be on the straight of the grain but the bulk in the centre will be greater and it will be more difficult to cover the centre neatly except with very fine fabrics. The joins in the fabric—paragraphs (b) and (e) above—should fall under a pleat.

To Complete

When all the cover has been stitched to the frame, the struts to which the panels

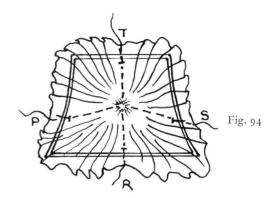

Fig. 94

have been stitched and the centres of the two ruched panels are neatened. The struts are best neatened by strips of self material cut on the true cross of the material $1''$ wide. The two raw edges are ironed in and the strip stitched to the cover (Figures 27a, b). The stitches with this type of material should be on the extreme edge of the strip and they must be minute.

The central trimming must be delicate; a motif of Guipure lace or a covered button or a trimming made by coiling commercial braid if this is used for neatening the rings. Insert the internal lining and stitch well to the outside of the rings so that the stitches are covered by the trimming of the rings.

Suggested Quantities Shade Plate 11c.
Base $12''$, height $6\frac{1}{2}''$.
   Ruched panels and lining of these panels:
      $\frac{3}{4}$yd. $44''$ chiffon.
   End panels: $\frac{1}{4}$yd. $36''$ material.
   Internal Lining: $\frac{1}{4}$yd. $36''$ material.
   1yd. trimming for four struts.
   2yds. trimming for the rings.

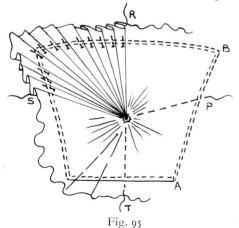

Fig. 95

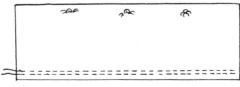

Fig. 96

17

Shade with Sun-ray Pleated Panels [Plate 11(b)]

THIS IS A form of pleating which is very suitable for panelled shades. The pleats radiate from a point midway along the bottom of one panel (Figure 99). Plate 11b shows a shade with four panels pleated in this way separated by four cut-a-way corners to which a textured material has been fitted. On other shades only two panels may have this pleating.

Again the choice of style of frame is important; this form of pleating is not suitable for shades which have panels with a concave curve. The pleats would jump across such curves and the shape of the frame would be altered.

These shades may have an internal or external lining depending on the style of the frame. The struts to which material is to be stitched should be bound and if an external lining only is to be used all the struts are better bound to match this lining.

MATERIALS

Shade with 10" base, height 6½"(As Plate 11b).

1yd. of chiffon or georgette: 4 strips 9" × 36".

½yd. lining.

4 pieces of material 4" × 8" for the cut corners.

2½yds. velvet ribbon (to trim the 8 struts and top ring).

1½yds. trimming for the lower ring.

3½yds. ¼" tape or ribbon for binding the struts.

2¾yds. ⅜" tape for the rings.

METHOD

Internal lining

This is fitted in a rather unusual way as the seams of the assembled lining are not placed to two struts, but to the midpoints of two panels. The lining is fitted on the straight cross of the fabric (Chapter 6, pages 27–30) but because of the shape of the frame it goes from the left-hand strut of one small panel to the diagonally opposite strut, which is, in fact, the left-hand strut of the opposite small panel (Page 26).

After it has been assembled it is re-inserted but the tops of the seams go to the midpoints of two of the larger panels and these points are usually at the junctions of the fitting and the top ring. The lower ends of the seam are then pinned to the midpoints of the same panels but on the lower ring.

Cover

The pleating on each panel is worked in two sections with a join at the centre line, MN. This enables the pleats to be balanced about the centre line of the shade, as in the shade in Chapter 14. To estimate the quantity of material measure around the two sides

68

and top edge of the panel. Double this length plus $2\frac{1}{2}''$ to give the total length of the strip and the height of the strip is the distance of N from A plus $2''$ for ease of working (Figure 97).

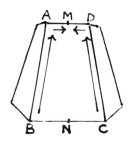

Fig. 97

1. Tear the material for each panel into two strips as shown in Figure 98 below. This length of strip will give spaced pleating at the edges of the panel.

2. Run two rows of gathering threads; one $\frac{1}{8}''$, the other $\frac{1}{4}''$ from the lower edge of each strip (Figure 98).

On the longer strip the gathering should begin $\frac{1}{2}''$ from the right-hand edge of the strip (Figure 98). This $\frac{1}{2}''$ will form a box pleat up the centre of the panel and it will cover the join of the two halves of the material. Use a strong gathering thread.

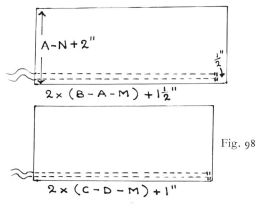

Fig. 98

3. Draw up the gathering threads very tightly and secure the ends.

4. Using the smaller strip of chiffon pin the gathers to the midpoint of the lower ring. They should come up to the point N but will extend a little to the right of the actual midpoint, i.e. from N to F, this distance should be as small as possible.

5. Pin the short end of the strip along the right half of the lower edge of the panel—from F to C (Figure 99).

6. Fit the ungathered long edge from C to M as spaced pleats (see Chapter 11). The raw edge will be covered later. Stitch to the frame.

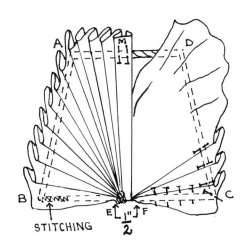

Fig. 99

7. Place the longer strip to the left half of the panel leaving the extreme right edge (i.e. the $\frac{1}{2}''$ without gathers) free at N.

8. Pleat along the left side BA and the top edge AM.

9. Turn in the end $\frac{1}{4}''$ of the free material and make a box pleat up the centre of the shade (Figure 99). Stitch to the frame.

10. Fit the other pleated panels in a similar way and trim away any surplus material from the struts.

11. Fit the corner fabric to the frame, pinning it first to the bottom ring and tightening to the top ring. Finally pin it to the two struts, this material should be quite taut. Stitch to the frame and trim. This is fitted on the straight of the grain.

12. Insert the lining. Fit the tops of the seams (see page 68 for method) then pin the tailor tack line (Figures 42 and 43) to the top ring. Pin the lower ends of the seams and tighten the lining (Chapter 6, pages 32 and 33).

Trimming

13. Trim the struts to which material has been stitched. $\frac{3}{8}''$ ribbon, strips of self material, or a narrow braid may be used. Attach the braid first to the top of the strut, tighten it to the bottom and secure to the lower end of the strut. The tightness will help it to curve round the strut, and at the same time ensure that it remains perfectly straight. Now anchor the trimming to the strut using the diagonal stitch (Figures 27a, b).

14. Trim the two rings. A motif of Guipure lace can be attached to the midpoints of each large panel to cover the gathers if necessary. Care is needed when taking the ring trimming over the ends of the strut trimming; bulk must be avoided but the ends of the braid on the struts must be completely covered.

N.B. In some shades similar to the one described above, the corners are in the shape of concave curves. These are fitted exactly as the panels on the shade in Chapter 9.

1. Types of Lining

Back row: (a) External lining, struts bound to match.
(b) Gathered lining, fitted to the lower ring—gathered at the top of the ring.

Middle row: (c) Lining of the cover fabric used on a coolie frame.
(d) Tailored lining in an oval drum.
(c) Pleated lining of white Jap silk under a dark cover

Front row: (f) and (g) External lining in candle shades, struts bound to match.

2A. Tailored Shades on Bowed Frames.
(a) and (c) bowed drums: (b) bowed empire.

2B. Tailored Shades.
(a) Oval drum with cover of red corded velvet and opaque interlining:
(b) shows the fitting of opaque lining for a panel: (c) petalled drum.

3. Set of Wall Light Shades
fitted on the straight of the fabric with design centralised.

4. Matching Table Lamp and Pendant Shade
intended for use in a cloakroom with a low ceiling.

5. Set of Matching Shades
used for six years and frequently washed.

6. Matching pair of Shades.

(a) panelled shade of Jap silk: (b) Jap silk of (a) used for lining and picking up a colour of the cover fabric.

74

7. Illustrating the variations of treatment possible on one frame.

8. Various collared Shades and methods of finish.

9. Fluted Drum Shades.
(a) Touching vertical pleats: (b) Fan pleating.

10A. Shades illustrating various methods of pleating, swathing and gathering.

10B. Further designs of pleating.

Back row: (a) Diagonal pleating: (b) Cross swathing.

Front Row: (c) Spaced pleats of white chiffon over deep pink lining: (d) Cross pleating over the end panels—shows untrimmed struts: (e) Honeycomb pleating using pearls to anchor the pleats and matching pearl trimming.

11. Three Bedroom Shades.
(a) and (b) using textured nylon and pleating:
(c) shade with central ruching.

12. Tiffany Shades
(a) Tailored cover in 4 sections. Shows untrimmed struts and external lining
—see Plate 25 for completed shade.
(b) Shade with gathered cover of Swiss cotton.

78

13. Group of shades for use in one room showing variation in the employment of colour and texture. (a) Green wild silk and glazed chintz panels: (b) Green chiffon: (c) Matching green chiffon with chintz panels.

14. Children's shades. (a) Acrylic paints on buckram: (b) Roundabout shade: (c) Wallpaper motifs on buckram with terylene top-cover decorated with Fabricrayons: (d) Curtain material on Parbond.

15. Painted and Dyed covers.
(a) Fabricrayons: (b) Batik: (c) Tie-dye panels

16. Pleated shade
using transparency of
cathedral window for
the central panel—
washable.

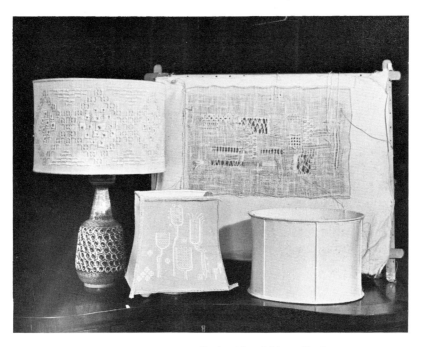

17. Embroidered Linen Shades.
(a) Tailored Cover: (b) Panelled Cover showing braids to be used for neatening: (c) Planning a cover using cut-work and pulled-work.

18. Shades using dried flowers and foliage.
(a) on acetate.
(b) on Parbond.

19. Covers using Bobbin Lace or Crochet.
(a) Lace panel and trimming: (b) Crochet cover—2 panels: (c) Crochet panel and trimming: (d) Lace edging and collar.

20. Patchwork Shades.

(a) Mounted over parchment: (b) Showing fitting of central panels.

21. Drum Shades.

(a) Buckram Christmas Shade: (b) Macramé Shade with orange lining and orange beads: also card of macramé plaits: (c) Using weaving threads over slub cotton mounted on Selapar.

22. Firm Shades.

(a) Paper Sculpture: (b) Scroll Shade: (c) Lantern Shade.

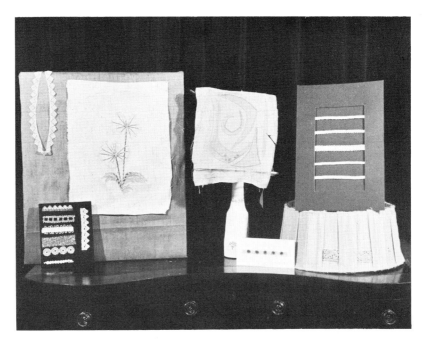

23. Embroidered Panels and home-made trimmings.

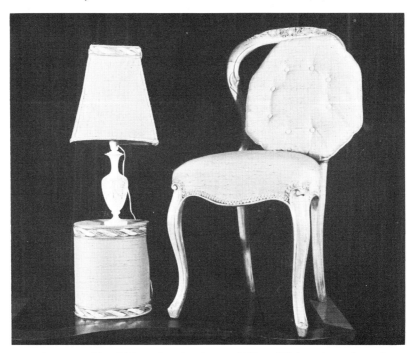

24. A group of furnishings showing the possibility of linkage in a scheme for a room.

84

25. A bedroom showing 2 lampshades covered by the same fabric as the bed-head and drapes.

18

Fan-pleated Shade [Plate 9(b)]

THIS IS yet another variation of pleating —usually worked in two colours or two shades of one colour. It can be worked very successfully on a shade with a fluted lower ring but this is not essential. If a shade can be found with a collar (Figure 5c) it will produce a very attractive, well balanced shade. The collar can be finished with either a wide decorative ribbon (Plate 8) which picks up the colours of the chiffon, or it can be covered with a band of touching pleats using the darker chiffon of the smaller fans. In this case both rings require trimming.

MATERIALS

Chiffon and georgette again are the ideal materials for the pleated cover, and crêpe-backed satin for the lining.

Suggested Quantities
Shade (Figure 5c)
    Circumference of scalloped lower ring 42″ (Diameter 12″)
    Length of strut 9″.
    Depth of collar $1\frac{1}{4}$″.
    1 yd. of paler chiffon for the larger fans of spaced pleats.
    $\frac{2}{3}$yd. deeper chiffon for the small fans of touching pleats.
    4yds. $\frac{3}{8}$″ tape for the rings.
    $\frac{2}{3}$yd. satin for the lining.
    $\frac{1}{2}$yd. ribbon for collar (optional).
    $1\frac{1}{4}$yds. trimming for the lower ring.

86

METHOD

Paint the frame and bind the rings (2 or 3).

1. Divide the paler chiffon into six or eight sections depending on the number of struts, i.e. one for each panel. Each panel should be twice the length of the section to be covered plus $\frac{1}{4}$″–$\frac{1}{2}$″ and the height should be 2″ more than the deepest part of the panel.

2. On the lower ring mark $\frac{1}{2}$″ in from the ends of two adjacent struts B and C, i.e. points X and Y. The lighter fan will fit into this section (Figure 100).

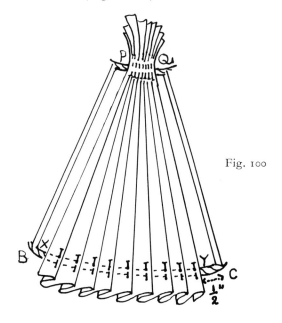

Fig. 100

3. Decide the depth of the pleats: $\frac{1}{4}''$, $\frac{3}{8}''$, or $\frac{1}{2}''$. Turn in this width of material and pin the fold to Y.

4. Continue pinning the material along the lower ring only forming spaced pleats (Chapter 11 and Figures 66–68). The last full pleat should be at X and the raw edge extend the width of a pleat beyond—this raw edge will be covered by the first pleat of the adjacent darker fan.

5. Mark the midpoint of the panel on the lower ring of the collar or on the top ring if there is no collar. Mark $\frac{1}{2}''$ either side of this point—P and Q (Figure 100).

6. Return to point Y and continue the fold of the material and pin to the top of the shade (Q).

7. Bring all the pleats from the lower ring to the top ring and they must all fit into the space PQ ($1''$) with only the raw edge extending beyond P.

8. Commencing $\frac{1}{2}''$ to the left of Q stitch the top of the pleats to the frame, the material here will be quite thick and the stitches must go through into the binding—use stab-stitch if necessary. The first few pleats are left unstitched to permit the raw edge of the last fan to be placed under the first pleat of this fan.

9. Adjust the pleats on the lower ring if necessary and stitch to the ring, again leaving the first pleat unstitched.

10. Fit the smaller fan of the darker fabric to the left of the fan already attached. This will radiate from $1''$ on the lower ring ($\frac{1}{2}''$ on either side of the strut at B). At the top these pleats will go from the top of the pale fan to within $\frac{1}{2}''$ of the midpoint of the next panel Q2 (Figure 101). These pleats should be $\frac{1}{4}''$ pleats and should be touching pleats (Figure 70). See paragraphs 11–13 below.

11. Tear a strip of the darker material

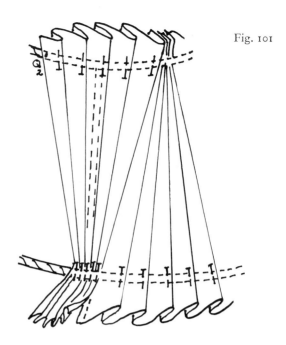

Fig. 101

equal to three times the distance to be covered. Turn under $\frac{1}{4}''$ on one short end and pin so that the fold covers the raw edge of the previous fan (i.e. pin the fold to P).

12. Pin touching pleats of $\frac{1}{4}''$ along this ring to within $\frac{1}{2}''$ of the next midpoint (paragraph 10). Again leave $\frac{1}{4}''$ of fabric to be covered by the next light fan.

13. Bring these pleats to the lower ring, all the pleats to fit into $1''$ (Figure 101). Stitch the pleats to the lower ring. Adjust the top of the pleats and stitch to the frame.

14. Continue to fit alternately light and dark fans until the last dark fan is reached.

15. Fit this last fan but tuck the raw edge under the first pleat of the first pale fan (paragraphs 8 and 9).

16. Cover the collar with touching pleats—if desired—see page 86.

The Lining

If the shade has no collar the lining can be fitted as that for a tailored shade (Chapter 6) or for a fluted drum (Chapter 12, Figures 75–77). If there is a collar the lining can be fitted as for the Pleated Empire Shade (Chapter 13, Figures 78–80). It is important to keep the stitching of the lining to the top or even outside the ring so the stitches can be hidden by the trimming. Neaten the slashes at the fittings with neateners.

To Finish with a Ribbon Collar (Plate 24).

This is covered after the lining has been attached. Fit a band of the lining material to the outside of the collar, overlapping the ends but not turning in the raw edge as this will be covered. Stitch the material to both rings of the collar (see page 55). Trim the lower edge back to the stitches, roll back the top edge and neaten (Figure 24). Fit a band of wide ribbon—wrong side out—around the collar. Remove and stitch the join. Trim the seam and replace the ribbon right side out. The ribbon should be sufficiently wide to completely cover the collar and just roll over the top edge of the ring. Stitch the ribbon into position, the join matching the join in the lining.

If the collar is to be covered by touching pleats both rings of the collar will require trimming.

88

19

Bed-head Shade

MATERIALS

1 bed-head frame (Figure 4f).
$\frac{1}{3}$yd. 36″ material for the cover.
$\frac{1}{3}$yd. 36″ material for the lining, if used.
$2\frac{1}{2}$yds. trimming.
6yds. of binding.
1 asbestos mat.

METHOD

This shade is very unusual as it is the only type of shade where the FITTING is bound. This binding avoids the metal of the frame scratching a polished headboard. The binding of the fitting should be overlapped more than the binding used on rings to give a thicker binding and so extra binding material must be allowed. Another extra is a piece of asbestos, which is covered and attached to the inside of the frame at the back. This acts as an insulator and prevents the heat from the bulb blistering the polished wood behind the shade.

This style of shade cannot, because of its shape, have an internal lining, and so where a lining is used it must be fitted to the outside of the frame.

1. Bind the frame with material to match the lining (if one is being used) or the underside of the cover fabric. Where a lining is used the cover and lining can be fitted and attached as one material.

2. Fit the material to the front of the frame. Commence by pinning the fabric along the top straight edge AD, taking care that the grain runs along the wire, otherwise the material will wrinkle when it is tightened across the curved section of the shade (Figures 102 and 103).

3. Pin down the curved strut AB, again with the grain following the line of the strut.

4. Pin down the strut DC, tightening against the strut AB, i.e. parallel to the straight strut AD (Figure 102).

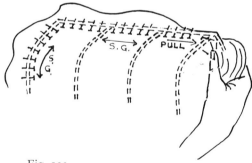

Fig. 102

5. Finally pin along the lower edge. No tightening must take place at this stage or the curved outline will be lost.

6. Stitch the material to the frame and trim away any surplus material from the struts AB and DC.

7. Fit the material over the two end panels keeping it very taut. Pin first down the back strut AF and then along the bottom edge FB. The grain will run along both these struts. Then pin the material to the curved strut AB. Stitch the panel to the frame and trim AB and AF. Fit the opposite panel.

8. Prepare the asbestos pad. Cut the asbestos so that the rectangle will just fit inside the section of the frame PFEQ.

9. Cut two pieces of lining material or of the cover the size of the asbestos plus $\frac{1}{2}''$ turnings. Tack these together, right sides facing each other.

10. Machine the cover along two long sides and one short side. Trim the seams to $\frac{1}{4}''$ and turn the material right side outwards.

11. Slip the asbestos inside the cover, turn in the seam allowance along the open end after trimming it to $\frac{1}{4}''$. Close the opening by overstitching the edges together.

12. Anchor this pad to the strut PQ—a few stitches at each end will suffice.

13. Fit the cover to the back section PQEF. Note that the small rectangle APQD is left uncovered—this allows air to circulate freely and so prevent scorching of the cover. Trim away any surplus material from the sides of the back panel.

14. Roll back the untrimmed material along the bottom edge, and the struts AD and PQ, and neaten (Figure 24). If a cover and lining are being used trim the cover before rolling back the lining (to avoid bulk).

Trimming

Here several edges have to be neatened and this should be done in the following order:
(i) strut PQ.
(ii) strut AD.
(iii) the ends B to A to F, and C to D to E.
(iv) the lower edge: F to B to C to E to F.

Variation

The front panel may be fitted in three sections. The panels ABHG and KLCD can each be fitted separately in the same way as the whole panel (paragraphs 2–6, page 89). The centre panel can then be fitted with a gathered or pleated panel. The pleats would be horizontal and the pleating would be started from the bottom edge.

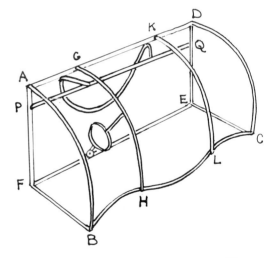

Fig. 103

20

Tiffany Shades [Plates 12 & 19(d)]

THIS IS one of the more modern shapes and reflects the current popularity of Victoriana. Even though it has been with us only a short time, variations on this line are already appearing in the shops. Figure 5d illustrates this trend to develop the original Tiffany shape.

It is a frame which allows for several treatments—some very simple, others while giving a simple tailored shade require more skill and care in fitting and attaching the cover. The simplest cover is a cylinder of material with a channel running along both the top and bottom edges. Into each channel is inserted either a length of tape or elastic as described below. These covers can be removed for laundering. More sophisticated ones are fitted so that all, or practically all, the fullness is removed at the top ring and the cover stitched to the frame. This type of cover must be fitted in two or more panels, depending on the suppleness of the fabric —Plate 12a was made from four panels.

Materials

As the frame recalls the Victorian era, Victorian-type materials, such as embroidered cottons and lacy fabrics, are particularly popular for the ruched type of cover—Plate 12b.

For the tailored type of cover, because of the very pronounced curving of the frame, it is very important that the material chosen should have plenty of 'give' so that the fullness near the top ring can be dispersed.

Preparation of the Frame

The frame is first painted unless bought ready prepared. With this type of frame it is impossible to fit an internal lining. As this type of shade has a large lower ring the struts are very conspicuous and so the painting must be very well done and the colour of paint used must match the underside of the cover perfectly. This may be an example of a shade where the struts are better bound with a matching material—see page 8, paragraph (b). If the cover is to be attached in panels then some of the struts must be bound and in this case it is advisable to bind all if the paint available is not a perfect match.

REMOVABLE COVER

To make a Removable Cover

1. Prepare the frame by painting only.
2. Cut a strip of material as shown in Figures 104 and 104a. The length of the strip is the circumference of the frame at its widest part plus $\frac{1}{2}''$ for the seam. $1''$ is allowed for the top channel and $1\frac{1}{2}''-2\frac{1}{2}''$ for the bottom channel depending on the size of the shade and the amount which is to roll over the bottom of the frame. The wider the channel at the bottom of the shade the less light will come from the shade.

91

To Make up the Cover

1. Join the two short ends of the material together—either by a French seam or a single seam with neatened edges.

2. At the top edge turn in $\frac{1}{4}''$ for the first turning and $\frac{3}{4}''$ for the second. Tack this down and make a similar seam along the bottom edge of the fabric. Machine the hems and machine-stitch the edges of the channels (Figure 104b). This makes a flatter and neater channel when the elastic is inserted. Leave $\frac{1}{4}''$ unstitched on each hem so that the elastic can be inserted.

3. Thread the elastic through the lower channel, draw up slightly and tie with a bow. Thread the elastic through the top channel and draw up quite tightly and tie up temporarily.

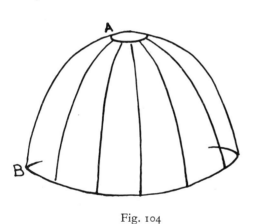

Fig. 104

4. Slip the cover onto the frame and anchor it to the frame with a few pins. These will have to be placed through the material and behind the rings as the rings are not bound.

5. Pull up the elastic in the top channel as tightly as possible and secure with a reef knot.

6. Draw up the elastic in the lower channel. This must be tight but it must be possible to stretch it sufficiently to remove it

from the frame. Secure the end of this elastic with a reef knot.

7. Remove the temporary pins. Take the shade cover from the shade and complete the stitching of the hems where the elastic was inserted. This stitching is preferably done by hand in case the elastic has to be removed.

8. Place the cover back onto the frame. A fringe may be stitched to the cover on the horizontal line through B if desired. This should be done before the elastic is inserted. In this case care must be taken that this line fits exactly on the ring of the frame. If round hat elastic is not available a narrow flat elastic can be used—this would be joined by overlapping the ends and stitching them together—not by tying a knot.

Fig. 104a

Fig. 104b

GATHERED COVER ATTACHED TO THE FRAME (Plate 12b).

This shade has a very much crisper and sharper line than the previous one. Since a soft fabric shade will wash successfully as a whole there is no particular virtue in having a removable cover on account of the laundering. There is a little extra work involved as the cover is stitched to the rings but the improved result usually justifies the effort.

To Work

1. Prepare the frame by painting and in addition bind both the rings.

2. Cut an oblong of fabric as in Figure 104a but only allow 1″ at the lower edge. No hem is made here, the extra inch is for working and neatening.

3. Join the two short ends with a French seam or a single seam with neatened edges.

4. Make a channel along the top long edge as in paragraph 2 of the previous shade. Insert a piece of elastic, draw this up slightly and tie with a bow.

5. With the right side of the cover outermost place it over the frame and pin the lower edge (i.e. the one with no channel) to the bound ring. Have the 1″ extra material below the ring. Stitch the material to the bottom edge of the ring. Roll back the surplus 1″ and neaten (Figure 24). Trim.

6. Tighten the top elastic as much as possible, tie with a reef knot and close the channel (paragraph 7, page 92).

7. Pin the material to the top ring, tightening against the bottom ring. The material will form concave curves between the struts and the top edge of the material will become slightly petalled, and both these effects are quite pleasing. Stitch the material to the top ring. The stitches will disappear into the gathers and there is no need for any trimming on this ring.

8. Trim the lower ring.

TAILORED COVER (Plate 12a)

This cover as its name suggests has no fullness at the rings, and so a material with plenty of 'give' is necessary. It has to be fitted in several panels. The shade in Plate 12a had 12 struts and the cover was in four panels, each covering three sections of the frame (Figure 105a) but involving four struts.

This shade may have an external lining and this would be fitted in exactly the same way as the cover—see below.

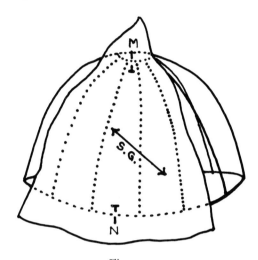

Fig. 105a

Preparation

Paint the frame to match the underside of the cover or the lining if one is used.

Bind at least those struts to which the panels are to be stitched, and since this shade has such a wide base and the struts are very obvious it is usually worth while to bind all the other struts. They should never stand out in contrast against the underside of the shade.

To Assemble

1. Place the material over a quarter of the frame and it must be on the true cross (Figure 105a).

The material is fitted with the right side of the fabric outside. Pin at M and N.

2. Smooth the material outwards towards the struts AB and CD. Pin at the top and bottom of each of these two struts.

3. Pin down the strut AB and then down DC, tightening the material across the frame (Figure 105b).

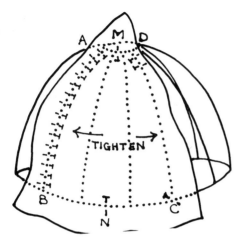

Fig. 105b

4. Pin along the two rings from A to D and B to C but do not overtighten between these two rings.

Almost certainly adjustments will have to be made to dispose of the last remaining fullness. At the corners of the panel this final tightening should be in a diagonal direction. Do NOT move pins M and N.

5. Stitch the panel to the frame keeping the stitches on the struts as small as possible to allow for neat trimming. The stitches on the rings should be on the outer edges.

6. Trim any surplus material away from the struts, cutting right back to the stitches.

7. Fit the other three panels, usually opposite panels are fitted first to avoid distorting the frame.

8. Roll back the surplus material at the rings and neaten (Figure 24).

Trimming

The four struts to which the panels have been stitched will need neatening. This should be kept as simple as possible and one of the most successful methods is to use crossway strips of the cover material. These should be cut $\frac{3}{4}''$–$1''$ wide. The two raw edges are folded into the centre (Figure 31). One strip is attached to the top ring at the end of the strut and then brought to the bottom ring keeping it as tight as possible, and then stitched. It will then grip the strut and further stitching should not be needed.

The top and bottom rings can be neatened with similar strips or a commercial trimming can be used.

Cover in Two Sections

With some materials which are very pliable it is possible to fit the cover in two sections instead of four. This also depends on the curve of the struts which varies from frame to frame.

TAILORED COVER ASSEMBLED BEFORE FITTING

As with the sectional cover this may be constructed from two or four pieces of material. It is necessary to check the frame to see if each of the twelve sections is identical—if not it will be necessary to fit each of the four sections separately, marking each quarter of the frame and the material which must return to it.

To Fit the Sections

The frame is prepared as for the previous shade, and the fitting is similar (paragraphs 1–4) except that the material is wrong side uppermost.

5. Mark along the fitting lines with pencil, tailor's chalk or by tacking thread. If using

a tacking marking take care not to catch the binding. Remove the pins. Trim as in Figure 106. If the frame is symmetrical a template may be made (see Chapter 8, Figures 56, 57) and used to cut the other three panels. If the frame is not symmetrical each quarter must be fitted separately.

6. Join the four sections with single seams. If the shade is not lined, then French seams should be used or single seams which are oversewn.

7. Line the shade with an external lining which is fitted and attached in the same way as the cover of the previous shade. Pages 93 and 94. The trimming away of the surplus fabric from the struts must be very neatly done.

8. Place the assembled cover over the lining, the seams being over the struts to which the lining was stitched. Pin into position and stitch to the two rings. Trim off surplus material and roll back the edges of the lining over the last row of stitches and neaten (Figure 24). The shade is now ready for trimming and on this shade only the two rings require a trimming.

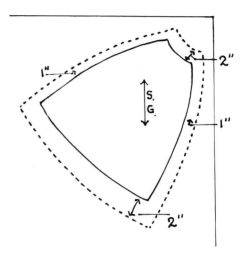

Fig. 106

21

Cone Shades from a Graph [Plate 14b]

THE TWO most popular firm shades are the cone and the drum, the latter being a development of the former—see below. As with any firm shade all that is necessary are two rings, one with a fitting and one plain, together with the cover fabric. The fact that this material is stiff prevents the shade from collapsing.

The proportions of the shade vary tremendously; a cone may be tall compared to the base ring to give a chimney shade or it may be shallow with a tiny top ring and a large bottom ring so giving a coolie shade. The choice is the worker's, depending on the position of the finished shade and the base on which it is to fit if it is a reading lamp.

TO DRAW THE GRAPH (Figure 107)

Use squared paper if possible or a set square, protractor or T-square will be necessary. Decide on the diameters of the two rings and the height of the shade.

1. Draw a line AB equal to the diameter of the lower ring.

2. Mark the mid-point of this line—C— and erect a perpendicular through C. If squared paper is used this is quite simple, otherwise use a set-square, protractor or T-square; it is essential that this line is at right angles to the line AB.

3. Mark on this line from C the vertical height of the shade—CT—this is not the length of the sloping side of the shade.

4. Through T draw a horizontal line again using a protractor or set-square if necessary. On this line mark P and Q, PQ being the diameter of the top ring and T its midpoint.

5. Join A–P and continue this line until it meets the line through C and T, the intersection of these lines is O.

6. Join B–Q; if the graph is correct this line when extended will pass through O.

7. With centre O and radius OA draw an arc which will pass through B.

8. With centre O and radius OP draw an arc which will pass through Q.

9. Make a mark on the large ring and place this mark at A on the graph. Roll this ring along the inside of the outer arc, AB exten-

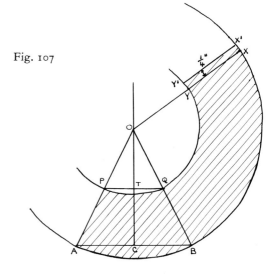

Fig. 107

96

ded, for one complete revolution, i.e. the mark will be back on the line-mark X. The ring, although on the inside of the arc, should be touching it as it is rolled along. Great care is needed at this stage.

10. Check the measurement by repeating the rolling of the ring, and by calculation, it should measure $3\frac{1}{7} \times$ AB.

11. Join X–O cutting the smaller arc at Y.

12. Starting at P roll the smaller ring for one revolution; if the graph is correct this should coincide with Y.

13. Draw the overlap Y^1–X^1 of $\frac{1}{4}''$.

The shaded section is now the complete graph.

N.B. If a pair of large compasses is available these can be used for drawing the arcs —if not, a simple means of doing so can be improvised. Either a strip of card or a tape-measure can be used. Many tape-measures have a metal end with a hole pierced in it; place a drawing pin through this hole or through the end of the card into the graph at point O. Mark off the position of A and rotate the tape or card pencilling the arc as the rotation proceeds (Figure 108). It is not wise to use a piece of string for this operation as this can stretch.

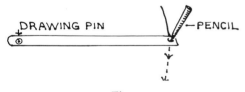

Fig. 108

It is always wise to check the graph before using it to cut out the firm material. It is very easy to get a slight inaccuracy in the rolling which will give a one-sided cone (Figure 109). This is a very common fault in this type of shade.

Cut out the graph in brown paper and fit

to the ring with as much care as with the final cover. If the shape is perfect cut out the firm cover; if not, check the graph—redrawing if necessary. If the firm material has a linear design or is made from a woven material bonded onto card care must be taken with the grain. The straight of the grain must be exactly opposite the join (Figure 110).

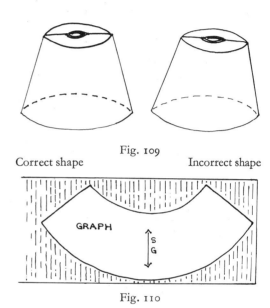

Fig. 109

Correct shape   Incorrect shape

GRAPH

Fig. 110

Preparation of the Rings

These are first painted and then bound with any of the materials listed on pages 9, 10 or 14. Bias-binding can be used on rings as extreme tightness is not so important as with soft-fabric shades; even so the binding should not slip on the rings.

When binding the ring with the fitting, always begin the binding at a junction of the fitting and the ring as it is easy to anchor the binding at this point. It is more difficult to commence the binding of the plain ring as the material tends to just slip round and round the wire. This problem can be solved by securing the binding to the ring with a spot of clear adhesive—this must be allowed to dry before starting the actual binding.

The binding is similar to that for the rings of frames with struts (Figures 12–14).

To Assemble

The lower ring is attached to the material first and it can be held in position with spring-type clothes pegs (Figure 114); pinning is not suitable as the tendency of the firm fabric is to spring back to become flat and so push out any pins holding it to the ring. The lower edge of the material should be just level with the bottom of the ring (Figure 111). Viewed horizontally the ring should not be visible (Figure 112a), neither should it be set in from the edge of the material (Figure 112b) or the edge will be bent during stitching and the smooth edge lost.

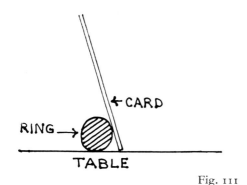

Fig. 111

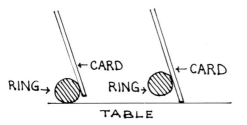

Fig. 112a & b

(a) Ring too low   (b) Ring too high

Stitching

The lower edge is now ready for stitching. The stitch used for soft fabric shades (Figures 23a, b) may be used, or, alternatively, a large running-stitch or stab-stitch (Figure 26). With the oversewing stitch the needle must pass through the material into the binding on the ring. If the reverse occurs, i.e. the needle comes out through the material, then this material is liable to be torn as strain is placed on the previous stitch (Figures 25a, b). Commence stitching about 1″ from the overlap, work round the shade and finally securely stitch the join at the rings.

Fix the top ring in position and stitch in a similar way.

The Join

This must be very even—the $\frac{1}{4}$″ allowed on the graph. The neatest result is obtained when the join is stuck with a clear adhesive such as clear Bostik, Uhu, or clear Evostick. The adhesive should not be applied direct from the tube; it is far too easy to have too much squeezed onto the shade also it is difficult to place it in the correct position. Squeeze a little onto a steel knitting needle or large darning needle and carefully rub this down the underside of the top of the overlap. To ensure a good join place the frame on its side with the join on a piece of polythene on a table. Put another piece of polythene inside the frame and hold the join firm with a weight. This ensures a flat join —free from any bulge and the polythene will peel off if any adhesive should escape from the overlap.

Trimming

Braids or other flat trimmings are most suitable for this type of shade (see Chapter 29).

To use Self-Bonding Parchments

Cut out the cone in the card after testing for a perfect fit (page 97). Place the material to be bonded over the card taking care that the grain is correctly placed (Figure 110). The material is then bonded to the parchment either by ironing or removing the protective sheath (see page 17). Cut out the material leaving an extra $\frac{1}{4}''$ at the overlap edge. The extra $\frac{1}{4}''$ can then be glued down to the reverse side of the parchment so preventing a white edge to the join. With commercially bonded material it is often possible to remove the firm material from the soft cover and a similar edge can be obtained but an extra $\frac{1}{4}''$ must be allowed in addition to that for the overlap.

Coarse Fabrics as Outer Cover

Sometimes it is required to use a thicker material such as hessian or a coarse linen as an outer cover over a cone shade. In this case the join, if worked in the above way would be very bulky. This problem can be overcome in the following way.

Make a cone shade as described above using a plain card, or clear acetate as the base.

Take the soft fabric and fit this, wrong side outwards, over the cone (Figure 113). The straight of the grain must run down the shade diametrically opposite the join (Figures 110 and 113). Pin the join of the fabric so that the material fits tightly to the basic cone (Figure 113). Slide the fabric sleeve off the shade and tack on the pin line. Machine with a small stitch.

Press the seam open—if the material is liable to fray seal the seam allowance with a clear adhesive and then trim both edges to $\frac{1}{4}''$. Replace the sleeve over the cone, matching the seam to the join of the card, and stitch it to the rings. Complete the shade with a suitable trimming.

Fig. 113 NOTE Straight grain of material exactly opposite the seam of the firm fabric.

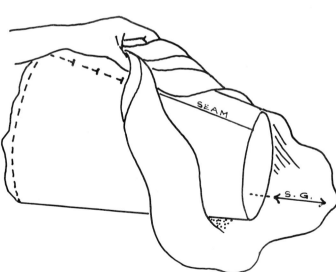

22

Firm Drum Shades [Plates 14, 18, 21a & c]

MATERIALS

TWO RINGS of equal diameter, one with a fitting—either pendant, recessed or gimbal, depending on the type of shade to be made—(Chapter 1, pages 3–4).

Binding materials for these rings—woven type if the cover is to be stitched into position or adhesive tape if the cover is to be stuck to the rings.

Firm material—the height according to choice—the length equal to the circumference of the rings plus $\frac{1}{4}''$ for overlap.

Clear adhesive.

Trimming for the two rings.

METHOD—STITCHED COVER

1. Bind the ring which has the fitting, commencing the binding at a junction of the fitting and the ring and securing the end of the binding to the beginning after the ring has been bound (Figure 19).

It is more difficult to commence binding the plain ring as there is no point to which the binding can be easily anchored and so it tends to slip around the ring. Anchor the tape to the ring with a spot of adhesive and when this is dry begin to bind—there will then be no difficulty.

2. Cut a rectangle the required size from the firm material. Make sure that the edges are cleanly cut and that the four corners are right angles (Figure 114a).

3. Fix the material around the rings using spring-type clothes-pegs to hold it in position (Figure 114b). Pins are not satisfactory here as the firm material tries to spring away from the rings pulling the pins from the binding.

4. Check that the overlap is quite even and trim if necessary.

5. Stitch the material to the rings using the oversewing stitch (Figures 23a, b, 25a, b) or stab-stitch (Figure 26) depending on the toughness of the material.

Commence the stitching $\frac{1}{2}''$ from the under edge of the overlap and finish by sewing through both layers of this overlap. Take care that the edge of the ring is level with the edge of the fabric (Figures 111 and 112).

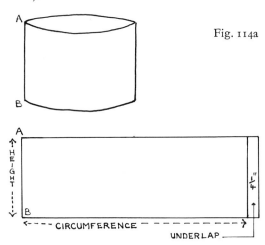

Fig. 114a

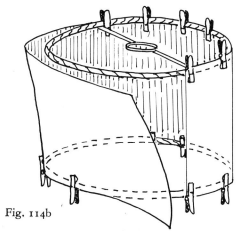

Fig. 114b

6. After both rings have been stitched to the material complete the vertical join by sticking the two layers together (see page 98).

Trimming

As these shades have no lining it is very important that the trimming rolls over the edge of the shade so hiding the binding of the rings.—See page 123. Usually a braid-type trimming is used with this style of shade, but again this is a matter of personal choice.

N.B. When using bonded materials it is possible to prevent the white edge of the cut card being visible.

With parbond or Selapar, after the material to be bonded has been fixed to the card trim the material to the shape of the card but leave an extra $\frac{1}{4}''$ at one short end. This is rolled over the cut edge and stuck to the back of the card.

If using one of the commercially bonded materials, cut the rectangle $\frac{1}{4}''$ longer than the suggested amount given in *Materials*, i.e. circumference plus $\frac{1}{2}''$. Carefully peel $\frac{1}{4}''$ of the soft fabric away from the background and cut away the extra $\frac{1}{4}''$ of this background. The soft material is then rolled to the back of the firm base as in the above paragraph.

This neatened edge is then the top one of the overlap.

VARIATIONS OF THIS SHADE
(Plates 14, 18, 21)

Shade I. Shade (18b) had pressed flowers as its decoration (see Chapter 28). The Parbond, with the black fabric and all the flowers (except those over the join) already in position, was stitched to the rings. In this shade $\frac{1}{2}''$ of the black material had been left along both long edges of the rectangle. $\frac{1}{8}''$ of the $\frac{1}{2}''$ had been pressed to the wrong side and the remaining $\frac{3}{8}''$ was rolled over the ring and stuck down after the stitching had been completed, so hiding the ring. A layer of clear acetate was then stitched over the shade using stab-stitch (Figure 26). The shade was then trimmed with crossway strips of the black material and a silver cord.

Shade II. The flowers of 18a were mounted on textured parchment and covered with a protective layer of acetate as in the above shade. Both rings were neatened on the inside with a white trimming which extended over the edge of each ring. A $\frac{3}{8}''$ velvet ribbon, which matched the petals, then was used to edge the top and bottom of the shade; it was not necessary for this to roll over the edge of the shade.

Plate 21c. This shade was made from adhesive card covered by a slub-textured cotton fabric. Weaving threads which had an interesting texture were then laid over the cotton. Each thread was secured to the upper and lower edge of the shade with a spot of adhesive. The inside of each ring was neatened with a white cotton trimming stuck into position. The outer edge was trimmed with velvet ribbon the same colour as the weaving thread.

Nursery Shades. Shade 21a was made completely with adhesive as it is not required to last any considerable time. The rings were bound with adhesive tape. Shades 14a and 21a used buckram as a base, it is inexpensive and easily obtainable. In 14c animals were cut out of wallpaper and attached to the buckram background. The rings here were bound with tape as a material (man-made fibre) over-cover was to be attached. The child and tree on the material were drawn with Finart Fabricrayons (Chapter 28, page 115).

This material was then fitted, wrong side out, around the shade (see Figure 113) and the two ends joined with a single seam. The seam was trimmed to $\frac{1}{8}''$ and the sleeve turned right side outermost. This was then slipped over the shade and stitched to the rings. The surplus material at the rings was rolled back and stitched (Figure 24) before being trimmed away. This shade is very attractive for children as the animals appear when the shade is lit up and they complete the picture.

The design on shade 14a was painted directly onto the buckram using fast-drying acrylic paints.

Plate 21a: Christmas Shade. This is a very seasonal shade so it is made as quickly and cheaply as possible. Buckram is used for the base which is stuck to the rings. These are neatened with a cotton braid and felt leaves and berries used to edge the shade. They could, alternatively, be arranged as a spray motif across the centre of the shade. The berries were punched out with a filing punch or a leather punch could be used. The leaves were edged with adhesive and then sprinkled with glitter.

TO ASSEMBLE WITH ADHESIVE

When using adhesive to fasten the cover to the rings it should be applied very sparingly to the outside of the bound ring. The cover should be released halfway round one ring (Figure 114b) and this half stuck to the ring and the pegs replaced while the other half is secured. The pegs should not be removed until the adhesive is quite dry. Both rings are secured and then the vertical join is finished as for the cone shade.

23

Merry-go-round Shade [Plate 14(b)]

MATERIALS

3 Rings; 1–3″ pendant ring.
            2–12″ plain rings.
$1\frac{1}{8}$yds. Selapar.
$1\frac{1}{8}$yds. Cotton fabric preferably with a texture such as a slub finish.
Oddments of fabric for the horses.
$2\frac{1}{4}$yds. cord or plait of macramé, etc.
$2\frac{1}{2}$yds. trimming for neatening the three rings.
Bondina.
5yds. $\frac{3}{8}$″ tape for binding the rings.
Clear adhesive.

METHOD

1. Draft a pattern for the upper half of the shade. This is a cone (see Figure 107). The measurements for this graph are:
    Diameter of the large ring 12″.
    Diameter of the small ring 3″.
    Height of the cone 3″.
Test the pattern for a perfect shape (page 97).

2. Make a pattern for the lower half of the shade (Figure 114a):
    Length = the circumference of the 12″ ring plus $\frac{1}{4}$″, i.e. 38″ (approx.).
    Height = 8″.
Test this for a good fit with $\frac{1}{4}$″ overlap; rings are not always perfectly true to measurement and to check at this stage can prevent wastage of material.

3. Cut both these patterns out from the Selapar but do not remove the protective film.

4. Iron the Bondina to the back of the fabrics to be used for the horse sections—following the instructions given by the Bondina under 'patching—(A) Body, (B) Tail, (C) Mane, (D) Saddle.

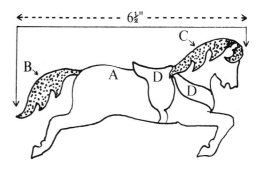

Fig. 115

Sections of the Horse Appliqué

5. Mark the outline of the oblong of Selapar very faintly on the right side of the cotton fabric and arrange the sections of the horses in position.

6. Having removed the skin from the back of the Bondina on the material to be used for the horses cut these out to the required shape, using the templates above (Figure 115).

7. Attach the various sections to the cotton background using an iron and a damp cloth as in the instructions.

It is essential that the cotton material is NOT attached to the Selapar before this stage or the steam will ruin the card.

8. Remove the protective film from the rectangle of Selapar and carefully place the marked cotton rectangle over it; the wrong side of the fabric to the sticky side of the card.

9. Trim away the surplus material but leave $\frac{1}{4}''$ on one short side to be rolled over the cut edge of the card and stuck down onto the back of the card (see page 99).

10. Peel the film from the cone section of the card and attach the cotton fabric to it, taking care that the grain of the material is correctly placed (Figure 110).

11. Cut out the cone from the cotton material, again leaving $\frac{1}{4}''$ on one edge to be folded to the back of the card.

N.B. Care must be taken that the same edge of both pieces of Selapar, e.g. the right-hand edge has the fabric rolled over it to give a continuity up the join of the assembled shade.

TO ASSEMBLE THE SHADE

12. Make up the cone as in Chapter 21 using the 3″ ring and one 12″ ring, but in this case have the lower ring slightly protruding below the edge of the covered card, as is shown in Figure 112a. This allows the lower drum section of the shade to be attached to the same ring.

13. Fit and stitch the rectangle to the other 12″ ring taking care that the overlap faces the same way as on the cone (paragraph 11 above).

14. Fasten the top edge of the drum section to the lower ring of the cone section with adhesive. When this is dry strengthen the join by stitching with stab-stitch.

15. Join the seam of the drum section with adhesive (see page 98).

Trimming

Choose either a suitable commercial or home-made cotton trimming to neaten the top and bottom rings, also the join of the cone and drum sections.

Attach this trimming to the shade with the clear adhesive (see page 123). Prepare the cords to go from the saddle to the top ring. Because these cords are liable to unravel they may be knotted at each end; this prevents the unravelling and is at the same time decorative. The cords are then stuck into position.

Variations

This shade can be adapted in many ways. Motifs can be cut out of furnishing fabrics with a nursery design and these used instead of the horses. Plain wallpaper can be used instead of the cotton base and paper animals or transfers can be stuck onto the background.

24

Scroll Shade [Plate 22(b)]

MATERIALS

1—8″ recessed ring.
16—8″ squares of firm material or
32—8″ squares of non-reversible material.
1 strip of material 1″ × 26″.
Binding tape.
Clear adhesive.

This is a quickly made shade, as the work consists almost entirely of sticking the sections together.

The choice of material is rather limited on two accounts:

(a) both surfaces are visible therefore both sides of the material must be attractive. With materials patterned on one side only two squares must be used for each section thus doubling the cost.

(b) no bonded material is suitable if it is liable to fray.

One of the most successful materials is textured parchment; it is easy to use and is attractive when viewed from either side so it can be used single thickness.

If, as is preferable with some fibreglass materials, two squares have to be used for each scroll the inner one should be slightly smaller but it is easier to trim it after the scroll has been made. The two squares are stuck together with a spot of adhesive in the centre—not around the edges.

METHOD

1. Bind the ring with woven tape or adhesive tape.

2. Stick or stitch the 1″ strip of parchment around the ring, the ring being in the middle of the strip. Trim the overlap to $\frac{1}{2}$″ and secure the join with a few small stitches.

3. Mark each square as shown in Figure 116.

4. Slash along the solid lines PX and QY.

5. Roll the square and slot the two slashes into each other (Figure 117).

6. With a spot of adhesive at the midpoint of each scroll—point O—attach it to the strip of parchment around the ring.

No trimming is necessary with this shade. The light transmitted by this shade is quite interesting as there are three different densities in the various areas of the shade.

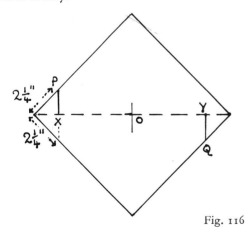

Fig. 116

Fig. 117

25

Paper Sculpture Shade [Plate 22(a)]

MATERIALS

2 rings: 1 plain; 1 recessed or with gimbal. Both rings to have the same diameter.

1 strip of parchment or decorative card, to measure $1\frac{1}{12} \times$ the circumference of the rings in length and $12\frac{1}{2}''$–$13\frac{1}{2}''$ in height according to choice.

Polyvil (PVC) tape or Tex-a-tape or Masking tape to bind the rings.

Clear adhesive.

METHOD

1. Cover the rings with the adhesive tape (page 14, Figures 20a, b, c).

2. Cut the parchment to shape, taking care that it is a true rectangle (Figure 118).

3. Mark off along the top and bottom edges of the parchment a length equal to the circumference of the rings—do not cut off the surplus.

4. Divide these lengths into twelve equal parts and mark on both edges (Figure 118) A, C, E . . . B, D, F . . . Join the opposite points, i.e. A to B, etc. All lines must be drawn very faintly.

5. Draw the line PQ $1''$ from the top edge, to cut CD at L^1–GH at K^1, etc.

6. Make a template of the diamond (Figure 119).

7. Place this diamond on the construction line CD with the top point of the template at L^1 and draw round it.

Repeat on the line GH with the top point

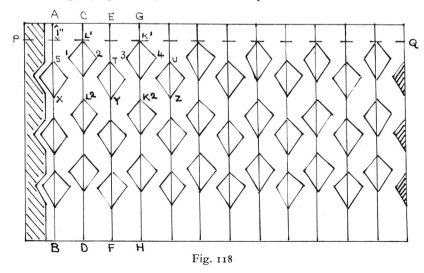

Fig. 118

of the template at K^1, and so on on every alternate construction line.

8. Place a long ruler through the points 1, 2, 3, 4 . . . and mark each point where it crosses the intervening construction lines AB, EF . . . at S^1, T^1, etc (Figure 118).

9. Place the template with the top point at S and draw the outline. Repeat at T then U and continue (Figure 118).

10. Complete the drawing as Figure 118. The last row of diamonds should be $1\frac{1}{4}''$ or $2\frac{1}{4}''$ from the lower edge according to the depth of the parchment—see above. L_2, K_2 are on the line through X, Y, Z, etc.

To create the Openwork

11. Using a sharp penknife or Stanley knife cut through the card along the two top edges of each diamond (Figure 120b).

12. Working on the right side of the parchment score on the continuous lines (Figure 120). Care is needed when scoring the card NOT to cut right through it (Figure 121a, b).

13. Working on the wrong side of the parchment score on the dotted lines (Figure 120a).

14. Fold the parchment away from the scoring (Figures 121a, b).

15. Trim both edges of the parchment by cutting away the shaded areas in Figure 118.

To Make up the Shade

This shade is made up as the 'Drum Shade by sticking' (pages 101–102). The right-hand side of the parchment in Figure 118 is the outside edge when the seam is finished. If this shade is assembled neatly and cleanly, no trimming is needed.

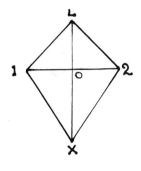

Fig. 119

$$1—2 = AC = \tfrac{1}{12} \text{ Circumference}$$
$$LO = \tfrac{1}{2}AC$$
$$OX = \tfrac{2}{3}AC$$

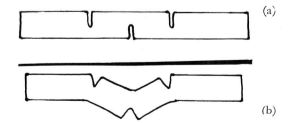

(a)

(b)

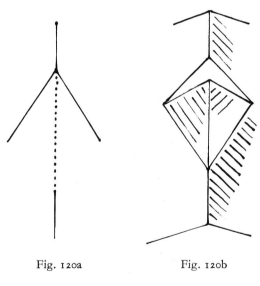

Fig. 120a   Fig. 120b

Fig. 121 Cross-section of card showing (a) depth of scoring (b) how paper bends away from scored line

26

Lantern Shade [Plate 22(c)]

MATERIALS

    1 Plain ring 5″ diameter.
    1 ring, with recessed fitting, 5″ diameter.
    1 strip fabric 12″ × 16″.
    1 strip fabric 14″ × 16″.

When choosing the firm material for the outer cover it is important to select one which will not fray down the cut edges. This excludes many of the commercially or self-bonded materials where a woven material has been bonded onto the card base. The straw-cloths can be used usually without fear of fraying. Fibreglass, parchment or wallpaper bonded onto Selapar are all suitable for use as the outer cover. The inner cylinder can be a matching or contrasting one; either in colour or texture.

METHOD

    1. Prepare the two rings by binding with tape or bias, the binding chosen to match the material used for the inner cover.

    2. Take the smaller piece of material, which will be the inner cover, and fix the two long edges to the rings (Figure 114b). There will be an overlap, trim this to $\frac{1}{4}$″. Stitch the material to both rings.

    3. Stick the join (page 98).

    4. Prepare the second piece of material as in Figure 122.

    Check it for fit round the cylinder already assembled before marking the position of the slashes. This piece of material need not overlap as it will be stuck to the top and bottom of the under cover. Trim off any surplus material. Mark the position of the cuts very faintly with pencil.

    Divide the material into 21 equal sections of $\frac{3}{4}$″ approx. It may be necessary to make minor adjustments to the measurements if a thick material is being used for either of the covers. A 1″ border is left uncut along the top and bottom edges.

    N.B. The number of strips and their widths can be adjusted as desired.

    5. Cut through the vertical lines with a Stanley knife or paper cutting knife. Cut against a firm edge e.g. a steel ruler and over a thick wad of newspaper. A sharp knife is essential to obtain a clean cut.

    6. Using a clear adhesive attach the outer cover to the inner cylinder. Spread the top $\frac{1}{2}$″ of outer cover with adhesive and stick it to the top edge of the inner cover. Then spread the inside of the outer cover with adhesive along the lower $\frac{1}{2}$″. Push up this edge until it is level with the bottom of the inner cover. Hold the two covers together with paper clips or clothes-pegs until the adhesive is dry.

    7. If the cutting and assembly are neatly done, there is no need for a trimming to be used, but this is a matter of choice.

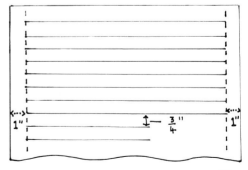

right
Fig. 122

108

27

Macramé Shade [Plate 21 (b)]

(Illustrations by G. N. Barke)

MATERIALS

1 8″ True-Drum Shade, round or oval.
2 balls of parcel string.
3yds. of ⅜″ tape.
¼yd. of lining material. (Optional)

This shade is very simple in design, but the effect is very attractive when the bulb is lit. It can be made without a lining and in that case the frame is simply painted and no binding is needed.

If, however, some colour is required in the shade a lining can be inserted after the macramé work is completed. In this case the two rings are bound with tape.

METHOD

Cut lengths of string, each one to measure eight times the height of the shade, plus the length of any fringe that is to neaten the lower ring. It is very important that these strings are sufficiently long to make any joining unnecessary.

Each length is folded in half. The loop is placed behind the ring and the two ends passed through the loop, so forming a knot, and securing the string to the frame (Figures 123a, b). Successive lengths are attached to

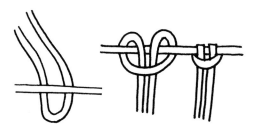

Fig. 123a   Fig. 123b

the top ring until it is completely covered. These knots must be pushed tightly together and the number of knots on each panel must be divisible by 2 (26 knots per panel in Plate 21).

To Work the Knots

1st Row: Take 4 ends (from 2 knots), pass the left-hand thread under the centre pair and over the right-hand thread (Figure 124a). Pick up the right-hand thread and pass it from front to back through the loop between the central pair and the left-hand thread. Tighten the threads firmly, this is the first half of the knot (Figure 124b).

2. Pass the right-hand thread under the central pair and over the left thread. Put the left thread, passing from front to back, through the loop between the central pair and the right-hand thread. Tighten firmly. This completes the knot (Figures 124c, d).

N.B. This flat knot is really a reef knot over a central pair of threads. To obtain an even tension the central threads must be kept very taut.

3. Continue working this knot round the ring (using four threads each time) until one complete row of knots has been worked.

2nd Row: Take the right-hand pair of threads from one knot on the first row together with the left-hand pair from the adjacent knot and work a complete knot. Continue until row is complete (Figure 125).

3rd Row: As the second row, but again moving two threads to the right for the first knot, thus a twill pattern is formed. If the same four threads were used for the knots in successive rows the result would be a series of disconnected cords.

When sufficient rows of knots have been worked to reach the bottom ring the threads are knotted to this lower ring. The worked cover should be stretched to reach the lower ring, or the shade will lose its shape.

To Knot the String to the Ring

Take two threads from one knot and pass the left thread round the ring to the left of itself, back to the front of the ring and thread it from right to left under itself (Figure 126). It will be necessary to thread the string through a coarse needle to accomplish this knot as there will be no space between the cover and the lower ring. The second thread of the pair is worked in the same way but taken to the right of itself (Figure 126).

The whole of the lower edge is secured and the ends of the string can be knotted to form a fringe.

LINED SHADE

If a lining is to be inserted this is made before the macramé work is begun. Both rings are bound and a pair of opposite struts are temporarily bound.

The lining is fitted and assembled as in Chapter 10, but not machined.

To Insert the Lining

After the macramé is completed, fit the lining to the inside of the shade and adjust the seams, trim to $\frac{1}{8}''$ and overcast them by hand or machine. Insert the lining as in Chapter 10, pinning to the inside of the rings. Stitch on the insides of the rings, the stitches passing between the knots into the binding tape.

Turn the surplus material on both rings to the inside of the shade and secure (Figure 24). Trim very finely. Neaten the inside of the shade with a macramé plait (Plate 21) on both rings.

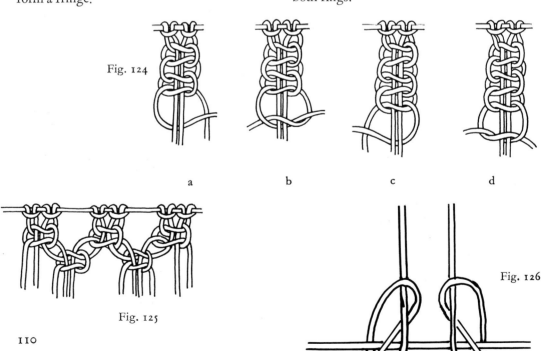

Fig. 124

a   b   c   d

Fig. 125

Fig. 126

28

Introducing Another Craft [Plates 14 ,15, 17, 18, 19, 20, 21 & 23]

THERE ARE so many skilled workers today who feel that they would like further outlets for their craft. Lampshade covers are surely a field for experiment. It is soon realised that certain limitations are imposed by the fact that the majority of shades have light transmitted through them, and also by the fact that covers are stretched tightly during fitting. These limitations should not however be a deterrent, but a challenge to be overcome. Certainly the results are very rewarding being both attractive and original.

Obviously a very wide range of crafts can be used, but given below are some which have been used successfully together with observations on problems which arose during working.

EMBROIDERY

It is not a new technique to use embroidery on lampshade fabrics but there are certain problems for which allowances must be made.

(a) Appliqué—any applied pieces must be laid exactly on the grain of the main material. If the grain of the two fabrics do run at an angle to each other then during the stretching which takes place while the cover is being fitted, the applied section may well bubble.

(b) Thought must be given to the effect of any threads taken from motif to motif on the back of the material. Those threads will be visible when the lamp is lit. Therefore either each motif or group of stitches should be complete on its own, or the threads passing from one group to the next should form an integral part of the design, although only visible when the bulb is lighted.

PULLED LINEN WORK

Thought must be given to the shape of the frame and the direction of the stretching during fitting. Any fitting on the cross may produce bubbling of the background and distortion of the design. A true drum, or a frame with panels, is the best choice. It should be possible for the grain to run parallel to the two rings of the frame. In this case the edges of at least one of them can be neatened before the cover is applied. The cover can then be blind-stitched to the bound rings. A fascinating effect of this type of cover is the design produced by the spaces and eyelet holes when the bulb is lit—this is quite as apparent as the threads used in the actual embroidery. With this type of cover an external lining is necessary.

A problem with many fabrics suitable for use in pulled linen embroidery is that they fray very easily. This can be difficult if the cover is applied in panels. To prevent fraying bond it to the external lining before stitching it to the frame. The pulled linen panel (Plate 17b) was backed with Jap silk by using Bondina. A thin material should be used for the lining to prevent bulk on the struts. This Jap silk or other fine fabric acts as an external lining and so the struts should be suitably bound or hidden by neatening strips. It is important in panelled shades to keep the stitching small so that a narrow trimming will cover the raw edges. This trimming should be in keeping with the embroidery. On drum shades the material can be made up by the method for lace-covered shades (Chapter 7).

DRAWN THREAD WORK (Plate 17c)

This is particularly effective as it allows light to be transmitted in varying densities, thus emphasising the design used. Again consideration must be given to the style of frame to be used before any threads are drawn. For a drum shade, where the tightening is in a vertical direction, horizontal threads must be withdrawn. For frames with bowed struts, and where the tightening is in a horizontal direction, then vertical threads can be cut and drawn. This type of cover demands an external lining, the shade may or may not have an internal or balloon lining as well. The external lining can be quite a strong colour, such as orange under lemon, again this emphasises the design of the embroidery.

Any trimming should be in keeping with the type of embroidery and a trimming made from the background material is usually to be preferred.

By choosing a variety of textures amongst the threads used in the embroidery, the interest of the resulting panel is increased.

ITALIAN QUILTING

This is a craft very often used when making cushion covers. If it is also used on panels of lampshades, again we have a tie up of various small articles of furnishing in the home. The quilting shows up very well when over a light. Care is needed when threading the quilting thread through the channels as the normal small loops cannot be left or they would show up as a shadow. It is preferable to use a thickish man-made yarn rather than the normal quilting wool, as this will not shrink.

A variation of this craft is to use the cording foot of a machine and a twin needle with a cotton thread under the fabric.

For both these methods, it is necessary to line the shade in order to hide the quilting threads and the muslin backing in the case of Italian Quilting.

English Traditional Quilting is also practical for panels, if a thin layer of synthetic wadding such as acrilan or terylene is used instead of the traditional wadding. Any surplus wadding should be trimmed away to avoid bulk at the struts. Even very thin, $\frac{1}{8}''$, non-inflammable foam can be used on large shades which is particularly effective under furnishing chintz, if part of the pattern is outlined with machine-stitching.

MACHINE EMBROIDERY

The same general rules apply to this craft as with hand embroidery. Use of twin needles, and single or twin hem-stitching needles on organdie, can be rewarding. Several layers of organdie can be used and then one or more cut away to give variation of the amount of light transmitted through the shade. The lining under this type of cover should be quite deep in tone.

BEAD EMBROIDERY

Here again thought must be given to the pattern which will be made by the threads joining the beads. These will be visible when

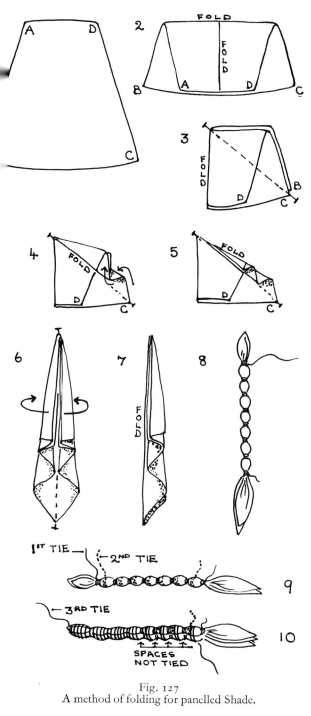

Fig. 127
A method of folding for panelled Shade.

the lamp is lit. They can be incorporated in the design, when the original planning is done. Individual beads must be attached singly very neatly and no ends left visible.

TIE-DYE PANELS (Figure 127, Plate 15c)

Jap silk is very suitable for tie-dye panels for lampshades, but equally well cotton lawn or any other fine fabric can be used subject to the dyer's instructions. If the fabric is too heavy the resulting pattern may be too large for most lampshades. It must be reasonably small so that a complete pattern will fit in each panel. The design in the illustrated shade was taken from a carpet pattern in order that the lampshade and carpet should have a common theme. By choosing a suitable dye for the fabric it is ensured that the shade can be washed when necessary. Thin Jap silk panels can be dyed in pairs. The folding for the Shade (Plate 15c) is shown in Figure 127. Carefully planned folding is essential to achieve the desired pattern. It is wise to make a trial panel first. Dygon bleach and Dylon hot water dyes are very successful.

BATIK (Plate 15b)

The most suitable materials used for this type of shade are again fine silk and cotton. The panels were fitted as for a tailored cover, and the outline marked by a tacking thread. This is essential as a pencil mark would be removed during the frequent washing during the processing. The design was drawn on paper in biro so that it could be seen through the silk during waxing. The wax acts as a resistant to the cold water dye, therefore, with careful planning, a design including several colours can be achieved. To remove the wax before the cover was assembled the material was pressed between layers of absorbent paper, and finally washed in a mild soap solution in hot water. Hot water dyes cannot be used or the wax would melt and be removed during processing. Dylon was found to be quite fast during the final washings to remove the wax.

FABRIC PAINTING

For the artistic, fabric paints open up a still wider field. The paint used could be either a specially prepared medium, e.g. Printex or an acrylic based paint. Very attractive results can be achieved by arranging leaves, etc., on fabric and then spraying the background with an acrylic paint with a spray diffuser, which can be bought from an art shop. Dylon have recently produced an additive which can be used with their cold water dyes with success—this is 'Dylon Paintex'. It is a thickener which can be added to their cold-water dyes for fabric painting.

DRIED FLOWERS (Plate 18)

This is a very impressive way of making a beautiful shade. Care must be taken when selecting the dried material that only those unaffected by heat are used. Yellow flowers and those with a papery texture are successful. The shallow drum had cream flowers and silver foliage arranged on black crêpe which had previously been mounted on parbond. It is important to arrange the whole shade before any sticking is begun. The final flowers of the last group were attached after the card had been stitched to the rings, as they were over the join.

The tall drum was decorated with bougainvillaea petals, clematis stems and foliage, and helichrysium buds. These were arranged on textured parchment.

If larger dried flowers are used the shade may be sprayed with clear lacquer, but the life of the shade will be limited.

After the dried material has been placed in position, each piece should be attached with an adhesive such as clear Bostik or Evostick, and the adhesive applied with a pin. In no case should it be applied direct from the tube, or any excess may mark the background.

Any shade relying on this form of decoration would be very vulnerable to damage if the flowers were left exposed. To overcome this the shade has an outer cover of clear acetate. Apart from providing protection this can also be wiped down with a damp cloth as the whole frame cannot be washed.

The decoration of these shades must be very simple. The colouring and the arrangement should make the impact and the decoration should merely neaten and edge the whole shade.

PATCHWORK (Plate 20)

This was probably the most fascinating experiment. It appeared initially that the patchwork panels would have to be opaque with the light reflected from the shade by a pale lining. When however one panel was placed over a light with no dark interlining it became apparent that the turnings made a secondary design showing through the top fabric.

This gives an option of treatment, the shade can either have opaque panels or it can allow the light to be uniformly transmitted through all the panels. If the turnings are to be visible obviously they must be kept very even. Again, because of stretching when fitting the cover, care must be taken in keeping the grain of all pieces, running in one direction.

LACE (Plates 19a, d)

Bobbin Lace. This craft is enjoying a tremendous revival of interest, and it can well be used in panels for shades or even for some styles of shades for the whole cover. It can be set in linen panels and fitted over an external lining of a fairly strong colour (see pulled and drawn linen covers). If used with linen or fabric panels of any kind care must be given to match the textures. In the lace and linen shades rows of drawn threads were hemstitched to lighten the texture of the linen panels (Plate 19a).

The choice of pattern is important, e.g. when large spiders are part of the design care must be taken to keep them held centrally in the surrounding ground. It is extremely easy to pull them out of position and shape. A firm and wide edge ($\frac{1}{8}''$–$\frac{1}{4}''$) on both edges of a lace panel is necessary to allow for neat and firm attachment to any side material. If whole panels of lace are being used then the edge to fit to the rings must be self-neatening and have a decorative edge. In this case the lampshade can be made up and neatened without the lace cover, with external lining or external and internal lining. The lace can then be slid over the shade and attached with blind stitching to both edges using a soft invisible nylon thread.

If a separate lace edging is used as in the oval drum (Plate 19a) a narrow edging of the lining fabric can be used underneath it, otherwise it would be lost against the cover of similar colour.

CROCHET (Plates 19b, c)

This again can be used in the same ways as lace. The shade with a complete cover of crochet (Plate 19b) had a lining fitted and all the strut lines marked. The outline and strut lines were transferred to graph paper and the pattern built up. The edge was part of the design, rolled over the top ring, but was allowed to stand down below the bottom edge.

Crochet panels can be used exactly as the lace panels referred to above (Plate 19c).

It is important to consider tension, because much crochet applied to lampshades is too slack and soon becomes untidy due to loss of texture.

There are other crafts, such as tatting and smocking, which can well be used as fields for exploration for the adventurous.

FABRIC-CRAYONS (Plates 14c and 15a)

There is on the market a type of crayon known as Finart Fabricrayons which can be used to produce designs on various materials. They are most successful used on man-made fabrics. The design is drawn, first on paper, and then transferred by ironing to the background material. This again provides a means of linking various articles of furnishings as the design can be taken from the curtain material, wallpaper or the carpet used in a room. It is important to get the correct thickness of crayon on the paper; too little will give a pale colour, too much may cause spitting which will leave irremovable spots on the fabric.

29

Trimmings [Plates 17, 19, 21 & 23]

IT COULD well be maintained that no process in the making of a lampshade is more important than the first or the last. The initial skill—the binding of the frame, and in particular of the rings—lays the foundation of success, while the choice and attaching of the trimming adds the final touch of quality to the work. The importance of this final process cannot be over emphasised.

The function of a trimming is twofold:

(a) it must conceal any stitches or raw edges previously visible,

(b) it must give a final touch of decoration.

The trimming chosen should be suitable in colour, texture, design and weight to be used with the fabric of the cover of the shade. Trimmings with a silky finish can ruin the effect if used with some cotton, linen or other matt-surfaced fabrics. Guipure lace is a good choice to neaten shades covered with broderie anglaise (Plate 3).

Care is needed when deciding the colour of the trimming—a contrast is better than a poor match. It must be remembered, however, that some dark-coloured trimmings are not colour-fast and a shade can be ruined during washing if dye runs into a pale cover or lining. Advice should be sought regarding the fastness of the colour when buying the braid and even then a little of the braid should be tested before use.

Fashions change in the types of trimmings popular at any time as well as in the styles of frames. Braids, embroidered ribbons and metallic-type laces are popular at the present time rather than bobbles, tassels and fringes. This is very true of the trimming of the many firm shades which are made today. Long fringes have, however, enjoyed a revival with the popularity of the tiffany styles. The final choice is nevertheless purely personal, depending on the worker's preference, the style of the shade and its environment when finished.

One factor of supreme importance is the aptness of the trimming chosen to the style of the frame and of the cover. On some shades the trimming should be functional but unobtrusive, on others it may be the dominant feature of the shade. The former usually applies when it is necessary to neaten struts to which panels have been sewn. Very often (Plates 11, 13a 13c) these panels are decorative and the centres of interest and so the trimming must not detract from them. Narrow ribbon or strips of self-material are very suitable in such cases. Plate 24 shows a shade, very simple in line and treatment—here the trimming is an extremely attractive ribbon attached to the collar of the frame and it is the focal interest of the shade. It picks up the colour of the cover, together with other colours in the room, and at the same time neatens the top of the shade. The trimming of the lower edge was deliberately kept very simple; a strip of self-material, machine-stitched (Figure 137) in self-colour with just a narrow gold cord—as used in gold-work—to bring the gold thread in the ribbon to the base of the shade and so keep a good balance.

Pleated shades can be neatened with one of the many gold or silver laces that are available today, often these are combined with a narrow ($\frac{3}{8}''$) velvet ribbon. Frequently these lace edgings are of an open texture and used by themselves would reveal the stitching and maybe frayed edges. The addition of the narrow ribbon prevents this. It will be seen when applying the trimming how important it is to keep the neatening stitches (Figure 24) very shallow and the trimming very neat. If a broad trimming has to be used to cover up the finishing it may give the shade a heavy appearance.

On the shade in Plate 5 it was necessary, as it was a coolie frame, to use a deep tassel to prevent the bottom of the electric bulb being lower than the bottom edge of the shade.

$\frac{3}{8}''$ velvet ribbon is a most successful aid for using around the rings; it washes, it is wide enough to cover up raw edges and stitches, yet is sufficiently narrow to be worked round a curved edge without puckers appearing. $\frac{1}{4}''$ is rather too narrow to neaten efficiently whereas it is difficult to use $\frac{1}{2}''$ ribbon on a curved frame if it has to roll over the ring as is usually necessary: puckers appear on the edge and inside the ring.

With shades where the cover is pleated chiffon or georgette, strips of self-material can be used with a lace instead of the ribbon; as in Plate 13c. This is most useful: it is economical and a perfect match of colour is assured. Because of the texture of these materials the strips can be cut or torn on the straight of the fabric and used without difficulty. Selvedges of these fabrics are more opaque than the main piece of the material,

so are excellent for neatening. If there is insufficient selvedge to go round both rings strips of the material can be used double. If the top edge of the lace is to be covered, anchor this edge only with an oversewing stitch. The lace will sit on the outside of the frame and the ribbon or strip of material roll over the ring, so covering the stitches.

When using more substantial material (Plates 2A(a), 13a) the strips must be cut on the true cross so that they will grip around the rings. Such strips should always be fitted fairly tight so that they have to be stretched, after joining, when they are replaced onto the rings of the shade. One edge of these strips may be folded under before stitching to the shade, the other will be neatened when the strip is rolled over the ring (Figure 128a).

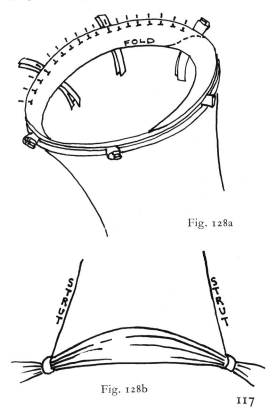

FOLD

Fig. 128a

STRUT   STRUT

Fig. 128b

Strips for neatening struts may be cut on the straight or the cross depending on the texture and the design of the material. If, on any of these strips, the ironed-back edges refuse to lie down they can be bonded down with thin strips of Bondina. With large shades (Plate 15b) wider strips of cross-way material can be used. They may be single with a decorative edge as in Figures 134–136 or they may be double as in the above shade. The raw edges are stitched to the inside of the shade (Figure 128a) and then the strip is rolled back to the outside of the shade and ruched with a narrow rouleau at the end of each strut (Figure 128b).

HOME-MADE TRIMMINGS

There are in specialist craft shops and department stores a vast selection of trimmings from which to choose but often it is preferable to make one's own. This is certainly more economical; it ensures a perfect match and the results will be original. They must, however, fulfil the functions of trimmings (page 116) but in addition they must be VERY well made. Badly made trimmings give a shade a 'home-made look' in the derogatory sense.

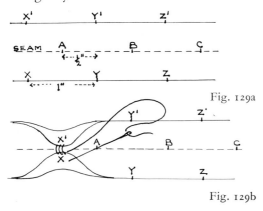

Fig. 129a

Fig. 129b

TYPES OF TRIMMINGS

Materials for these can include ribbon, net, self-material, macramé-twine, string, wool, weaving threads, crochet cotton, etc. The making of the actual trimmings can involve other crafts such as crochet, tatting, bobbin lace, plaiting, etc; the need of each particular shade is the factor to consider.

Fly-Stitch Rouleau

This can be made from a length of fairly stiff ribbon $\frac{3}{4}''$–$1''$ wide or from a tube or rouleau of self-fabric (machine-stitched) $\frac{3}{4}''$–$1''$ wide. Different effects are obtained according to the stiffness of the fabric being used. If a tube of material is being used, this should first be flattened so that the seam is in the middle of the flattened tube (Figure 129a).

(a) Mark the tube or ribbon faintly, as shown in Figure 129a, X–Y = Y–Z = $1''$. A is halfway between XX^1 and YY^1, i.e. $\frac{1}{2}''$ from each. The marking is done on the right side of the strip, the seam being on the back if a rouleau is used.

(b) To work: Bring out a needle threaded with a matching thread on the lower edge at X and pick up point X^1. Draw these two points together and secure with two or three tiny stitches (Figure 129b).

(c) Carry the thread forward, either through the tube or along the back of the ribbon, $\frac{1}{2}''$ to point A (on the line of the seam or halfway up the ribbon). Draw up A to XX^1 and secure (Figure 129b, c).

(d) Carry the thread forward again to Y ($1''$ from X). Make a small stitch to prevent

Fig. 129c

this point being drawn up to A. Draw together Y and Y¹ and secure. Pick up B and
draw up to YY¹. Continue in this way until
sufficient trimming has been made. The join
should be made to give continuity of design,
the actual join being made with ladder stitch.

Shell Ruching

Prepare a rouleau or tube from crossway
strips as for the Fly-Stitch Rouleau. The
width can vary according to the size of the
shade. After the rouleau has been turned
right side outwards it should be flattened so
that the seam runs down the centre (Figure
130a). The tube is held with the seam to the
front while the shell edging is worked.

To Work. Bring the needle out on the
seam and loop the thread round the rouleau.
Pick up a small piece of the tube almost
where the thread came out (Figure 130a).
Tighten the thread and secure with another
small stitch (Figure 130b). Run the needle
through the tube and bring it out $\frac{1}{4}''$ to $\frac{1}{2}''$
to the left of the last stitch, according to the
size of the shell required (Figure 130c).

N.B. Ribbon is not suitable for this trimming.

Petal Ruching

Prepare a rouleau as for the previous
trimmings or use a fairly stiff ribbon.

Commencing at one edge of the ribbon
work diagonal rows of gathering stitches
backwards and forwards across the ribbon
(Figure 131a). Care must be taken to keep
the angles of the rows even, so that the
distance between the points is uniform. Equal
care must be taken when drawing up the
gathering thread to obtain an even trimming
(Figure 131b). The ends of this type of
trimming can be joined before beginning the
gathering which is then drawn up so that
the trimming fits the frame.

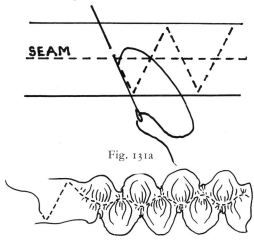

Fig. 131a

Fig. 131b

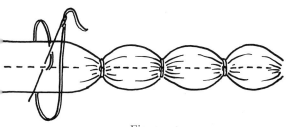

Fig. 130a

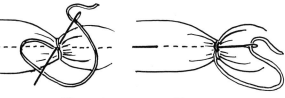

Fig. 130b   Fig. 130c

Box-Pleated Edgings

(i) *Touching pleats.* This edging can be made from ribbon or self-material. When using self-material, if this is fairly stiff, it can be used single thickness in which case the raw edge can be neatened with a narrow hemmer (Figure 134) or by hand, e.g. by a scalloped edge. If the material is delicate it should be used double.

To Work. Allow three times the circumference of the ring when calculating the amount of material necessary. Pleat as in Figure 132a, and machine through the centre of the trimming on the dotted line. For shades of 10″ or less the pleats can be $\frac{1}{2}$″ or $\frac{3}{4}$″ but on larger shades larger pleats can be made and the material used can be wider.

(ii) *Butterfly pleats.* These can be made from any of the materials suitable for the box-pleat edging. If, however, double material is being used, instead of using a wide strip folded to give the two thicknesses two narrower strips of different colours can be used to give a variation of effect or to pick up two colours used in the cover fabric. When the two strips have been stitched together the tube must be turned and pressed with care to get a clean edge. This is not necessary if using two strips of ribbon.

To Work. It is worked initially exactly as the box pleats (Figure 132a) but the pleats must be a little longer: $\frac{3}{4}$″–1″. The midpoints of each pleat are then caught together with two or three tiny stitches or possibly a bead (Figure 132b).

Laid edges

Here there is ample scope for experiment, both in the design which is built up or in the range of threads which can be used. Knitting and weaving wools, string, macramé twine and thick embroidery threads are all suitable, but should be in keeping with the particular fabric of the cover. It is easier to handle if the threads are couched down on a matching ribbon; there are then no problems of the couching threads showing on the inside of the shade. The ribbon is then attached as an ordinary trimming (Figure 133).

Use of Embroidery edges

These edges usually make use of strips of self-material. The raw edges can be rolled and whipped by hand or scalloping can be used to neaten the edges.

A comparatively new means of producing decorative edges is the swing-needle machine. With softer fabrics it will probably be more successful to use double material but a trial piece should always be made first. To improve finish of these edges it may be advisable to back the strip of fabric with Vylene or Staflex before working the embroidery.

A wide range of threads can be used;

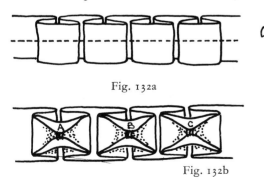

Fig. 132a

Fig. 132b

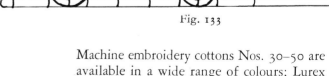

Fig. 133

Machine embroidery cottons Nos. 30–50 are available in a wide range of colours; Lurex threads and thicker embroidery threads can be used on the spool of the machine.

Some of the most successful of the machine attachments and stitches include,

(i) *the narrow hemmer* (Figure 134). This can be used on one or both edges of a strip of fabric to produce a simple trimming. It can be used with metal laces (page 117).

(ii) *the blind hemmer* (Figure 136). This produces the effect of shell hemming and so is an alternative to hand trimming which gives a shell edging. It is worked with double material, the bulk of which is kept on the right of the needle. Care must be taken that the needle, on its swing to the left, goes completely over the edge of the material in order to produce even shells.

(iii) *a scalloped edge* (Figure 135). This is a very useful finish but it needs careful trimming. With some machines it is possible to work the scallop over a thicker thread such as perle or crochet cotton and this gives a very firm edge.

(iv) *patterns* utilising the discs of the more versatile machines. Figure 137 shows an example of a very successful pattern; the two raw edges are trimmed and pressed to the back of the strip. If necessary these edges can be fastened down by using a very narrow strip of Bondina.

(v) *a disc pattern* can be embroidered with cotton or metal thread on a ribbon which is then attached as a braid.

Embroidered Edges

These are particularly suitable when using embroidered panels for the outer cover of a shade (Plates 17 and 23). Small patch-work shapes can be mounted on a ribbon to give an interesting result (Plate 23). This edging can be used on an otherwise plain shade. Pulled linen edgings are the ideal trimming for linen covers (page 112).

If a coarse fabric such as moygashel or linen has been used for the cover, strips can be frayed and hemstitched to give a fringe-type edge (Figure 138). Various adaptations of this type of edging are easily made, e.g. band of hemstitching can be worked in a strip of material to give a decorative braid or this braid can be combined with the above fringe.

Fig. 134

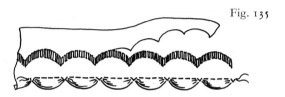

Fig. 135

Fig. 136

Fig. 137

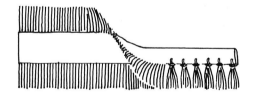

Fig. 138

Lace-Type Edgings (Plates 19, 23)

Bobbin lace, needle lace, tatting, mac-ramé, and crochet all can be used to produce inexpensive and original trimmings. It is important with this type of edging always to try a small length of the trimming to ensure that the tension is satisfactory, otherwise the trimming soon loses its crispness.

Crochet Trimmings

Abbreviations: ch., chain; d.c., double crochet; tr., treble; dbl. tr., double treble; cl., clusters; s.s., slip-stitch; to make a cluster work 3 or 4 dbl. tr. into the same stitch but leave the last loop of each stitch on the hook, pass the thread over the hook and draw it through all the loops, fasten the cluster with 1 ch.

Flower Edging (Plate 19c)

For the edging in the plate a No. 3½ crochet hook and No. 20 crochet cotton was used but these can be varied depending on how fine or coarse the trimming is to be.

1st Row. Commence with 5 ch. * Into 5th ch. from the hook work 3 dbl. tr., holding back on the hook the last loop of each dbl. tr., put thread over the hook and pull through all the loops on the hook (a cluster is made); 5 ch. repeat from * for the length required, having made an even number of clusters. Do not break off but work along one long side as follows:

2nd Row. 7 ch., make a 4 dbl. tr. cl. at the base of the last cluster of the 1st row, *7 ch., 1 d.c. at base of next cl., 7 ch., 4 dbl. tr. cl. at base of next cl., rep, from * ending with d.c. at base of the 1st. cl. of the previous row. Do not break off but work on the other side of the first row as follows:

3rd Row. 9 ch., 1 cl. into the same place as the cl. on the other side (i.e. of row 2). * 5 ch. 1 cl. into the same place as d.c. of

row 2, 5 ch., 1 cl. into the same place as cl. of other side, rep. from * ending with 5 ch.,† 1 dbl. tr. into top of the last cl. of the 1st row, 5 ch., turn.

4th Row. 1 tr. into 3rd. of 5 ch.,† at end of row 3.* 2 ch., 1 tr. into top of next cl., 2 ch., 1 tr., into 3rd of next 5 ch. Rep from * ending with 2 ch., miss 2 ch. of 9 ch. 1 tr. into next ch., 2 ch., 1 tr. into next ch., turn with 2 ch.

5th Row. *1 d.c. into 2 ch., 1 d.c. into next tr., rep. from* to the end of the row. Turn with 1 ch.

6th Row. 1 d.c. in each d.c. of Row 5.

The 2 rows of d.c. makes a narrow solid edge, extra rows of d.c. can be worked to make the braid as wide as necessary to cover any stitches and raw edges.

Opposite Edge. Join the thread at the end of the last cl. of the 1st row. * 8 d.c. over the 7 ch. of 2nd. row, 1 d.c. into top of cl., 3 ch., 1 s.s. into top of last d.c., 8 d.c. over next 7 ch., rep. from * to end of row. Fasten off.

Scalloped Edging

Make a length of ch. the required length. The number of ch. must be a multiple of 5 plus 2.

1st Row. 1 d.c. into 3rd. ch. from the hook, 1 d.c. into each ch. to the end of the row. Turn with 2 ch.

2nd Row. As row 1.

3rd Row. As row 1 without the last two ch. N.B. If a wider base is required to the trimming, work extra rows of d.c., otherwise proceed:

4th Row. 4 ch. (for 1st dbl. tr.), 3 dbl. tr. in 1st d.c. to form cl., 5 ch., 4 dbl. tr. cl., in the same (1st) d.c. (This makes a shell) * miss 4 d.c., 4 dbl. tr. cl. in the next d.c. 5 ch. 4 dbl. tr. cl. in the same d.c., rep. from * to end of row. Turn 2 ch.

5th Row. * 5 d.c. over the 5 ch. of previous

row, 1 d.c. in ch. between cls., rep. from * to end. Fasten off.

Fan-Edged Insertion

Make a length of chain the required length. The number of ch. must be a multiple of 4, plus 2 ch. to turn.

1st Row. 1 d.c. into the 3rd. ch. from the hook. 1 d.c. into each ch. to the end.

2nd Row. 4 ch. for 1st. dbl. tr., *1 ch., miss 1 d.c., 4 dbl. tr. cl. in next d.c., 1 ch., miss 1 d.c. 1 dbl. tr. in next d.c., rep. from * to the end.

3rd Row. 2 ch., *1 d.c. over the next ch., 1 d.c. in top of cl., I d.c. over next ch., 1 d.c. in dbl. tr., rep. from * ending with 1 d.c. in 4th. ch. from the end.

4th Row. 2 ch., 1 d.c. in 1st. d.c. (i.e. over dbl. tr.) * miss 1 d.c., 1 tr. 3 ch. 1 tr. all into next d.c., i.e. over cluster of row 2. Miss 1 d.c., 1 d.c. into next d.c. (over dbl. tr.), rep. from * ending with 1 d.c.

5th Row. Turn with 2 ch. 1 d.c. into 1st. d.c., *5 d.c. over 3 ch. of fan of previous row, 1 d.c. into d.c. between the fans, rep. from * to the end. Fasten off.

A ribbon is threaded through the 2nd row.

TO ATTACH THE TRIMMING TO THE SHADE

To stick or not to stick? This is often the question that is asked. The answer is usually quite simple—How was the shade made? If the shade has been made by sticking a firm material to the rings (Plate 21a), then the trimming can be stuck on. Even if the firm material has been stitched to the rings and further stitching is liable to tear the material, again the trimming should be stuck on. If the shade is to last for some considerable time and is likely to be washed, then it is sensible to stitch on any trimming. Usually a

trimming which has been sewn on is likely to withstand washing better than one which has been stuck and there is no fear of any adhesive discolouring. Even when a trimming has been stitched into position a little adhesive is used to seal the ends and so prevent them from fraying (Figure 141b), and it is important to choose one which will not discolour with heat or with the passage of time.

POSITION OF A TRIMMING

It must be remembered that the function of a trimming is to neaten; therefore it must be placed where it will achieve that aim. Rings are never attractive and so the trimming should obscure them if possible. With braid-type trimmings this is fairly easily done by allowing them to roll over the edge of the ring. This is very important when neatening the top ring of a table lamp where the top of the shade can be seen. If the selected trimming is not wide enough to do this, two widths, one inside and one outside, may be used. The two layers should be caught together along the top edge after they are attached. When two rows are used it is easier to attach the inner one first with a stab-stitch, the outer row is stitched with the usual stitch (Figures 27a, b) and so hides the other stitches anchoring the first row.

To achieve the rolling over the ring a braid-type trimming should be very tight and stretched around the frame; most braids will then roll naturally over the ring. Conversely a fringe-type edging must NOT be stretched around the frame or the pendant section will curve inwards and spoil the line. Hanging trimmings, e.g. tassels, etc., should be laid with the braid section on the shade and the pendant section hanging freely from the outside of the lower ring (Figures

139a, b). The braid section is then stitched as in Figures 27a and b.

TO JOIN THE TRIMMING

The method depends largely on the type and texture of the trimming. Those which are flat can be joined before they are stitched. If there is a definite pattern in the braid this should be matched so that the join is as inconspicuous as possible.

(1) *Flat Braid*

Place the braid, wrong side outermost, around the ring to be neatened, tightening quite firmly (Figure 140a). Pin the join and remove the braid from the shade. Back-stitch the seam, remembering to make any adjustments in order that the pattern shall match (Figure 140b). Trim the ends to $\frac{1}{8}''$ and, as these braids are very liable to fray, these ends should be sealed with a little adhesive applied with a pin (Figure 141b). Replace the braid around the ring making sure that it rolls over the top or the bottom of the ring. The seam in the braid should coincide with the seam of the cover, or in the case of pleated or gathered covers it should match the seam of the lining (Figure 140b).

(2) *Trimmings with Depth of Texture*

Some braids have quite a thick or fluffy texture and to make a seam in these would produce a very bulky join. Fit the trimming around the ring commencing at a seam (see above), but leave an extra $\frac{1}{2}''$ to be trimmed away just before joining the ends. This is because the end may fray during stitching. Stitch the braid into position (Figures 27a, b) until 2″ remains. Turn end back over the stitched braid and hold with a pin (Figure 141a) while the beginning is trimmed back to the seam line. Trim the second end so

124

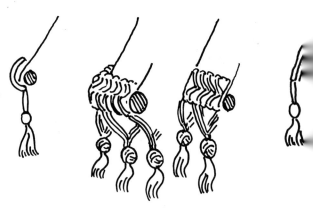

INCORRECT   CORRECT

Fig. 139a   Fig. 139b

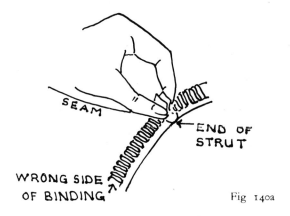

SEAM

WRONG SIDE OF BINDING

END OF STRUT

Fig 140a

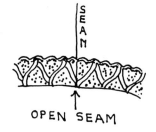

SEAM

OPEN SEAM

Fig. 140b

that the two ends just meet. Touch both ends with adhesive applied with a pin (Figure 141b) and then press them together and onto the shade. Use a needle or pair of scissors to press them into position, not the fingers (Figure 141c). The braid tends to stick to the fingers and will fray when the finger is removed, whereas it does not adhere so readily to metal. When the adhesive is quite dry complete the stitching.

(3) *Metallic Lace Trimmings*

These are more difficult to join. By virtue of their composition they tend to spring apart. They are however easy to adjust to obtain continuity of design. The actual join can be done as flat braid above and the ends stuck back on the main body of the lace. The ends should be left longer than $\frac{1}{8}''$ as it would be difficult to fasten such a short length back. An alternative method of joining is to overlap the two ends for one pattern and to stick the ends together. As these laces are usually used in conjunction with ribbon or narrow strips of self-material which rolls over the ring, the lace is attached

just below the edge of the ring and is not stretched.

(4) *Tassels, Fringes and Bobble Trimmings*

These are joined in sections. The braid section can be joined by methods 1 or 2 and it is not stretched before joining (page 123). Any joins required in the hanging sections are best done by sticking—allow a little overlap and apply small spots of adhesive.

When using a lace edging combined with either strips of self-material or velvet ribbon the lace is usually attached first. It is fixed just below the edge of the shade and caught with a slip-stitch along the outer edge only— i.e. the edge which will be covered by the strip of material. The strip of self-material is then fitted to the ring as a flat braid (Figures 140a, b) and the ends joined. It is then stitched to the inside of the ring (Figure 128a) and rolled over to the outside of the shade, so covering the outer edge of the lace. A ribbon is attached exactly as a flat braid.

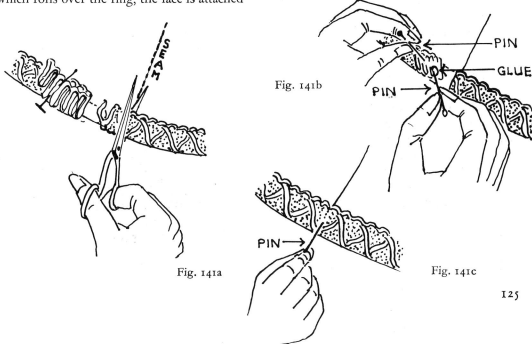

Fig. 141a

Fig. 141b

Fig. 141c

PIN

GLUE

PIN

PIN →

Useful Addresses

John Lewis & Co Ltd.
Oxford Street, London, W1 (also provincial towns)
Lampshade frames.
Firm Fabrics.
Woven Materials including wide range of chiffon, crêpe-backed satin, etc.

Dorothy Pye.
High Street, Moreton in Marsh.
Lampshade Materials and trimmings.
Unusual prints on Glazed Chintz.
Wide range frames (personal shoppers only).

Shade Crafts.
4 Park Street, Leamington Spa.
Lampshade Fabrics including crêpe-backed satin, georgette and chiffon.
Frames (personal shoppers only).

Arts & Crafts.
Green Lane, Derby.
Lampshade Materials and Frames.

Yvonne & Co,
17 King Street,
Leicester.

Hugh Griffiths.
Brookdale, Beckington, Bath.
Novelty Threads.

Mary Allen.
Turnditch, Derby.
Organdie.
Embroidery linens.
Embroidery threads.

Mace & Nairn.
89 Crane Street, Salisbury.
Gold Threads.

Distinctive Trimmings.
17 Kensington Church Street, Kensington, London W.8.
Trimmings of all descriptions.

Home Accessories Ltd,
The Lighting Centre,
35 Park Street
Bristol, 1

The Lampshade Supply Service,
26 Jordan Street,
Fulham, London.